D0500674

CEDAR MILL COMM LIBRARY
12505 NW CORNELL RD
PORTLAND, OR 97229
(503) 644-0043

WITHDRAWN
CEDAR MILL & BETHANY LIBRARIES

EVERYBODY IS AWFUL

(EXCEPT YOU!)

EVERYBODY IS AWFUL

(EXCEPT YOU!)

JIM FLORENTINE

DA CAPO PRESS

Copyright © 2018 by Jim Florentine

Hachette Book Group supports the right to free expression and the value of copyright. The purpose of copyright is to encourage writers and artists to produce the creative works that enrich our culture.

The scanning, uploading, and distribution of this book without permission is a theft of the author's intellectual property. If you would like permission to use material from the book (other than for review purposes), please contact permissions@hbgusa.com. Thank you for your support of the author's rights.

Da Capo Press

Hachette Book Group

1290 Avenue of the Americas, New York, NY 10104

www.dacapopress.com

@DaCapoPress; @DaCapoPR

Printed in the United States of America

First Edition: February 2018

Published by Da Capo Press, an imprint of Perseus Books, LLC, a subsidiary of Hachette Book Group, Inc.

The Hachette Speakers Bureau provides a wide range of authors for speaking events. To find out more, go to www.hachettespeakersbureau.com or call (866) 376-6591.

The publisher is not responsible for websites (or their content) that are not owned by the publisher.

Print book interior design by Jeff Williams.

Library of Congress Cataloging-in-Publication Data has been applied for.

ISBNs: 978-0-306-82563-7 (hardcover); 978-0-306-82564-4 (ebook)

LSC-C

10   9   8   7   6   5   4   3   2   1

CONTENTS

Foreword by Jim Norton   vii

PART ONE: AWFUL FACEBOOK

Chapter 1   The Education of an Awfulologist   2

Chapter 2   My First Prank Calls   15

Chapter 3   Construction Stories   35

Chapter 4   Strip Club Paradise   60

Chapter 5   Pranking Like It's 1999   76

Chapter 6   Florentine's Got Talent!   90

Chapter 7   *Crank Yankers:* The Early Years   112

PART TWO: AWFUL CONVERSATIONS

Chapter 8   Crazy Concert Stories   136

Chapter 9   Snuff Calls   153

CONTENTS

PART THREE: AWFUL RELATIONSHIPS

Chapter 10   Adventures in Home Abortions   170

Chapter 11   *Meet the Creeps*   188

Chapter 12   My First Murder Confession   207

Chapter 13   *That Metal Show*   223

Chapter 14   Acting Awful   237

The Awful Afterword   253

Acknowledgments   255

FOREWORD

"Yuck, what an asshole" was my first thought as I eyed up the guy across the room with long blond hair, ass gripping jeans and snake-skin boots. I was standing with NJ comedy booker Pat Gaynor in 1990, about one month into my comedy career. We were in a Spots-wood bar called The Varsity Pub, the place I did my first stand up set. Pat was giving me the rundown on the local open mic scene and suggesting where I might be able to get onstage. *"I'm going to intro-duce you to Jammin' Jim. He's a local comic from Old Bridge and will be able to help you get some stage time."* We walked towards the creep in the snakeskin boots, who looked like a Stonehenge rock in a Bette Midler wig.

"Jesus, he has throat cancer" was my second thought as Jim croaked out a *"Hey man, what's going on?"* in his trademark gravelly voice. I immediately realized my initial summation of this guy had been completely wrong. He didn't know me from a hole in the wall (and God knows I'm familiar with those), but he talked to me about com-edy and the local scene and started making suggestions as to where I could perform. He gave me his number and told me to get in touch about going on at the Playpen Lounge, a local strip club off Route

9 in New Jersey. Shockingly, a strip club off of Route 9 proved to be an awful place for comedy. I bombed there more often than not, but Jim always had something good to say, he'd always tell people about me and keep me in the loop about local open mics. I had nothing to offer in return, but Jim took care of me anyway. I was extremely unsure and vulnerable in those early days and he took me under his wing (and by wing I mean his giant scrotum) and introduced me to everyone. Most of the bookers hated me, I was doing jokes about fucking my grandmother in church and one of them even thought I was a Nazi.

I had expected him to be an aloof douche and he turned out to be one of the closest and longest lasting friends I've ever had in my life. I could write chapters on all of the great times we've had. In twenty-seven years, we've done countless gigs together, been to concerts together, acted together, pulled trains together, written pilots together, traveled together, lived together as well as seen each other through breakups, deaths and a never-ending list of career flops. So to narrow it down, I figured I'd list a few of the "firsts" I've experienced because of or with Jim Florentine.

The first time I got paid for doing comedy was because of Jim. In April of 1991, a local booker (the one who thought I was a Nazi) had a Holiday Inn gig that paid $25. Jim assured him I would do well and keep it fairly clean. Jim lied. I was a pig onstage and I bombed my fucking face off.

The first time I met a girl after a gig was because of Jim. It was some shithole in Connecticut and I was working with Jim and Bob Levy. After the show, a girl who looked mildly retarded was rubbing my leg under the table. I had never been more turned on in my life. It was the first time I might get laid *because of comedy*. I couldn't do anything with her due to the fact her brothers, who looked like linebackers on a prison football team, were cockblocking. Jim and Bob tried occupying her brothers by slowly rotating a shiny object in front of them as I attempted to sneak her into the parking lot. We didn't even need to have sex; I'd have been happy if she just gave me a kiss and threw rocks at my dick. Her brothers stood in the doorway and watched us, which of course ruined everything. On the way home, Jim was driving and Bob Levy was in the passenger seat. I masturbated in the backseat.

The first time I wrote a pilot was with Jim. We had both auditioned for a VH1 pilot called *Couch Potatoes* and miraculously, we both got it. They liked the idiotic chemistry we had together. The producers had us write all of our dialogue and our story line for the episode. I forget what we wrote, but I remember it was something about how we found the neighbors panties in the dryer and the gay couple upstairs was missing a gerbil. Very highbrow shit.

The first time I was ever in a movie was because of Jim. It was 1996 and the film was called *White Chicks Incorporated*. (*Worst Film Ever Made* must have been taken). Jim and Artie Fletcher played two losers who went to a witch doctor (played by white comedian Jeff Pirami). I played a successful, celebrity comedian. I was awful. And so was everyone else. But fuck it, it was a movie and it was my first and it wouldn't have happened if it weren't for Jim.

The first roommate I ever had was Jim. I lived at home until I was thirty. I was doing stand-up every night, but was spending all my money on prostitutes. I finally moved out of my parent's house and in with Jim and his girlfriend. We lived in Cliffside Park, New Jersey, and I was so happy to be on my own, I didn't realize the place was a cesspool. Three of us split $900 a month rent, and I just assumed that all cool bachelor pads were infested with silverfish, had rain water leaking into the living room and black mold openly growing on the walls. It was like living inside the asshole of a wild animal.

The first time I ever had a threesome with a buddy was with Jim. There was a woman I knew who was a really good egg and would have me over after her kids went to bed and blow on the sofa. She had a thing for long hair and one night I just brought Florentine over, figuring she'd be delighted to fellate him. She actually wound up blowing me while Jim had sex with her from behind, because my penis was wilting in shame and I knew if I tried have sex it would be a dismal failure. Jim, the consummate professional, maintained his erection and saved the day. The second guy I brought to see her was Rich Vos. Rich had sex with her and then walked outside like an asshole to smoke. She hated him.

The first time I met Ozzy Osbourne was because of Jim. He knew a guy named Frank who worked at MTV and Ozzy was being interviewed by some Russian host. Frank walked us backstage and we looked into the green room and saw Ozzy sitting there. I had no idea how to act, I was completely paralyzed. Jim played it cool and just talked to people like we belonged there and instead of following his cue, I just stood in front of Ozzy's door and stared at him like Boo Radley. Ozzy walked by us and I actually followed him to the bathroom to ask for an autograph. I didn't do photos back then, I typically just got people to sign my business card. We finally made it into the green room and as Ozzy is signing my card, Jim grumbled, "*Get the picture.*" I forgot he even had his camera. We snapped photos of each other with Ozzy, and thus began my twenty-year photo obsession. So for every celebrity who's had to throw their arm around my sloped shoulders and fake a smile, Jim is the guy to blame.

The first time I ejaculated on a television set was because of Jim. Bob Levy, Jim and myself had done a gig outside of Baltimore. All three of us were sharing a room, Bob the headliner in one bed, Jim and I in the other. (Jim's generosity once again. Neither of those guys had to let me stay in the room and Jim certainly didn't have to let me into his bed). After the gig, Jim was out sodomizing some waitress and Bob and I were smoking cigarettes in the room. Bob suggested we jack off on the TV so Jim could see it when he came back. I thought this was a fine idea. Bob went first, (when jerking off on the television, the headliner always goes first) and then I got up to the plate. I had a hard time getting going knowing one of my comedy heroes was laying in the bed behind me passing out with a Marlboro Light in his mouth. I forged ahead and finished. Then . . . we waited. We waited and smoked and finally, hours later, Jim came back in and saw the two loads on the television. He said, *"Beautiful"* and went to bed.

I don't even know where to end this because I love Jim so much and have spent so many of the most important moments of my life with him. There isn't enough room to write about when we waited on line to meet Black Sabbath, or when we flew to LA and I farted so much the flight attendant spritzed air freshener next to Jim's seat. Or about us performing at Woodstock 94, when we walked around in the huge performer tent and giggled at the giant penises bulging out of the shorts of the African musicians. Or about the time Jim talked his girlfriend and her friend into urinating on me. Or about the joy Jim expressed when Otto Petersen tracked dogshit into my new car. Unfortunately, this group of sophomoric, idiotic stories must wait to be told another day.

What I can say about Jim is I absolutely would not have made it as a comedian if it weren't for his friendship. And that no one can talk me off an emotional ledge like Jim Florentine. He is brilliantly funny and 100 percent original. Jim is probably the most genuine person I've ever met and has undoubtedly contributed more to my life than I have to his.

JIM NORTON
October 2017

Any woman that uses the word *kiddos* doesn't like to fuck.

—JIM FLORENTINE (2016)

AWFUL FACEBOOK

CHAPTER ONE

THE EDUCATION OF AN AWFULOLOGIST

I'm a simple man trying to live in a complicated world. Most days, all I want to do is maintain my peace of mind. But, that's hard as hell when everything I consider normal has flipped on its head.

All the rules have changed. Now, people broadcast their lives over the Internet instead of living them. Relationships are formed and lived out in cyberspace instead of real time. Conversations are had on smartphones where anyone with a shred of social media muscle can censor and troll you if they don't like what you are saying.

Let's face it; there isn't much room for a *simple* life anymore!

It's fucking brutal!

Being at odds with the way things are has caused me headaches, but it's also the source of almost everything I find funny. Believe me, there is a lot of awful shit that should not be. In a strange way, the stuff that frustrates the hell out of me has been the source of my comedy.

In fact, there are so many awful things to make fun of I've made a living out of it!

If you've followed my career, been to my shows, or heard my podcasts, you know I have fun raging against stupid shit. Sometimes the shit I deal with ruins my day but you guys enjoy me going off on it so it's all good.

That may be the silver lining! Laughing about our complicated world makes it easier to accept.

I wrote *Everybody Is Awful* for people like you. I know how annoyed you are with the drama in your life. I also know it's hard to find the humor in the bullshit awful people bring to our lives, but there is always something to laugh about when you look hard enough. Especially when you look at social media, or the crazy things that happen in relationships, or the stupid conversations we are forced to have throughout our day.

That's what this book is about!

I started the book by writing down the craziest stories from my career. While I was cataloging those insane moments, I discovered a backlog of frustration I needed to get off my chest. It's no surprise there was enough material to fill a whole book, the one you're now holding.

In the following pages, I'm going to ridicule the jerk-offs that foul up our good day.

I'm going to prove to you that everyone (except you) is truly awful! Laugh along as I rant and rave.

Maybe, if we're lucky, you'll learn to spot awful people and awful trends like the ice bucket challenge, Pokémon, or a new dumb Facebook game and avoid them at all costs. Maybe that will be enough to reclaim some peace of mind. Or, maybe that simple life will always be elusive, but if that's true, at least we can have some laughs while we look for it!

The Catholic Kid Goes Rogue

To start things off, let's go back to the beginning. I was an awful kid. How did I turn out this way? That's the big question.

Well, I've done about five minutes of serious analysis on this subject and I'm pretty sure it's my parents' fault. As a kid, my parents were super religious. While raising me, they had to depend on their faith and constantly prayed for divine intervention. You see, they had seven kids to raise and wanted to give us the best of everything.

Making sure we had a good education was important to my parents. Because they were Catholic, they made an unfortunate assumption that the local Catholic school could set me on the path to becoming a priest. There was one big problem with that—I don't like little boys.

Honestly, why does any parent think a school full of Catholic priests can offer a better education than a regular school? For instance, the school I attended had priests teaching sixth-grade math. How is a priest an expert in any subject other than religion?

Does counting how many kids you've *touched* give you special math skills?

How can a priest learn new math theories when they have so many inappropriate back rubs to give out? What would his math theory be? If I touch ten kids and no one says anything, did I really touch anyone?

Also, there was another reason I wanted to escape Catholic schools. All my friends were getting touched and the priests left me alone. I felt left out in a weird kind of way. Like most kids my age, I wanted to be with the rest of my friends, and they attended the local public school down the street. I begged my parents to transfer me but they wouldn't budge. So, since I couldn't get my way I rebelled—against everything!

There wasn't a rule I didn't bend, and there wasn't a piece of school property I didn't break! If that didn't work, I'd break the broken stuff until I was banished to the principal's office.

This resulted in me being grounded all the time. Most teenagers would love to be confined to their room so they could masturbate until they needed a life raft to float out of their room. For me, sex was the last thing on my mind because I was going to burn in hell if I did that. I treated my dick like it was a loaded gun. I was so afraid that even when I had to piss I'd try not to hold it because I was afraid it would go off accidentally. Making prank calls is all I wanted to do. Instead of studying or doing homework, I would use the landline in my room to practice my pranks.

I had no idea that my creepy misbehavior was forming the building blocks of a successful career. With an old rotary phone and a seriously demonic, I-don't-give-a-fuck attitude I was in the early stages of mastering my craft. I had just turned eleven years old, and I was on the way to becoming a professional comedian.

ANNOYING AIRPLANE ANNOUNCEMENTS

I just got off a flight going to Las Vegas. During the flight, the pilot gave us four different updates on the weather. I don't care about the weather when I go to Vegas. When I go there I go to drink, gamble on football games, and hope I have enough gas money to fill up my rent-a-car so I can drive out to the Bunny Ranch.

I don't care if the winds are six miles per hour out of the northwest. I'm not going to Vegas to fly a kite. Stop giving me an update on the weather!

At noon, we got the update:

"It's eighty-seven degrees and sunny right now in Las Vegas, I'll give you another update in an hour."

Why?

Why are you going to give me another update? What's it going to be, ninety in a couple of hours?

It doesn't make a difference. It's Vegas. It's August.

It's going to be fucking hot!

Part One: Awful Facebook

Facebook is fucking awful!

Does Facebook have any redeemable qualities? Does it do any good or just waste our time? For the most part, it fucking stinks! People are either bragging or looking for sympathy.

Pick a random place in your news feed and start reading, I guarantee that 99 percent of what you read will be meaningless junk news or annoying status updates, the kind that make you want to demolish your laptop with a sledgehammer.

If you doubt me about how awful Facebook has become, keep reading. I've got a shitload of examples that will convince you that finding a lump under your armpit might be better than reading one more fucking Facebook status update.

Awful Facebook Rule #1: Believe the Facebook Friend Fallacy

Over the last few years, fans of my podcast have sent me so many awful status updates I've become an expert in the shit that's posted. After sorting through all of them, I've found several horrible patterns. I took those patterns and converted them into what I call *The Eleven Rules for Being Awful on Facebook*. Here's the first one:

Believe that all of your Facebook friends are *real* friends!

That is the first rule for becoming an annoying dickhead on Facebook. If you follow this rule, you will feel empowered to spout off stupid shit all day, with no thought to what you are writing. You'll think that you have a legion of people depending on you to post every dumb thought that floats through your mind.

Also, you will expect every one of the poor souls to keep track of important events in your life, comment on all of your terrible pictures, love all the ridiculous memes you repost, and attend all your spontaneous gatherings. Your faith in Facebook friends makes you confident they have nothing better to do than be your best, most devoted friend. Nobody gives a fuck about your post of a rabbit eating from your dumb garden.

Friend Freak

For instance, look at the following post. This stupid cunt thinks she is Facebook royalty.

> Who says Facebook friends are not real friends? They enjoy seeing you on the internet every day, miss you when you're not on, show compassion when you lose someone you love, send you greetings on your birthday, view the pictures you upload, like your status, make you laugh when you are sad. Share this if you are grateful for your Facebook friends.

Then she writes . . .

> This is very true. Someone tell this to Mark Zuckerberg. He thinks Facebook is only for people who know each other in real life.

Guess what, dummy: Facebook friends are *not* real friends!

They're *not* going to be there when you need them. The only reason they wish you a happy birthday is that everyone else is posting that on your wall.

They feel *obligated*! They don't care. I promise you.

Nope, not one damn bit! If they did care, they would be at your front door with a fucking cake! And judging by your profile pic the last thing you need is cake.

My Dear Delusions

Here is another stupid bitch living out this Facebook friend fantasy . . .

> 🙂 I haven't even met many of my best Facebook friends in real life, but they are as dear as any I could ever hope for on here.

Are you fucking kidding me?

None of your followers said, "Oh, in three days, this chick in Seattle, who I've never met, is turning thirty-five. I need to make sure I don't forget. I'm buying my plane ticket now!"

The only reason they *liked* the dumb picture you posted is that they are just as bored as you are.

Share this if you're grateful for your Facebook friends, she writes.

But, nobody shared it and nobody should! I'd rather share a dirty needle with Charlie Sheen.

GARY FROM FLORIDA:
THE POLITICALLY INCORRECT SEXUAL SAVANT

Gary from Florida is a regular on my podcast *Comedy Metal Midgets*. He's a great friend and one of my most popular guests. Anytime I announce tour dates in Florida, I get swamped with emails asking if Gary will be at the show. He's in such demand he's even signed a few autographs after my gigs.

Gary is a slob! Yeah, he can come across as uneducated and offensive. But, the truth is Gary is an incredibly smart and decent guy. He's a respected businessman and he's made a lot of money in real estate. He loves to eat good food and drink great wine. But most of all, he likes to fuck women in the ass.

The reason my podcast listeners love him so much is because of his crazy stories about getting pussy. When he talks about his sexual adventures, he is absolutely politically incorrect. He always has crazy shit to share. A Gary-tale will either disgust you and make you want to run out of the room or it will mesmerize you so you hang on his every word.

What is his dirty secret to being such a great storyteller? *Gary is real!* He's one of the few people left in the world that isn't afraid to be themselves. He doesn't give a shit what people think of him! He's got big fucking nuts even when they aren't infected with ball wart. Most importantly, Gary from Florida is a Hall-of-Famer when it comes to getting women in bed and his years of experience and bold teaching style makes him one of the best sex gurus you've ever heard. You'll be happy to know, the following chapters have some of his best advice. Make sure you read every word! Your life won't be the same after that!

576 Reasons to Get the Fuck Off Facebook

Now, here is a woman who follows Rule #1 so fucking well, she has become certifiably delusional.

> Come hang out with me tonight at Sonny's restaurant for my early birthday celebration.

One hour later her friendship apocalypse starts . . .

> I have something to say. Out of the 576 friends, only one came out to celebrate my birthday with me. That says a lot about the 575 people that claim to be my friends. Wow! I'm crying and I'm in pain. W-T-F!

Ten minutes later, she's having a meltdown like an infant that needs a nap.

> 😠 This is the exact reason why I cannot be friends with anyone.

She thinks the 576 people in her friends list are her *real* friends. How many of those friends actually live in the area? How many can drop what they are doing to hang out with this disaster of a human being? Maybe fifty? Nevertheless, this woman expects everyone to be there. She thinks she's given enough notice so that all 576 *friends* can arrange to travel to her hometown just to hang out in a sports bar for her birthday. What a fucking dunce.

Out of her 576 Facebook friends maybe 10 care about her. The rest *never* even think about her because they *barely* know her!

Maybe a handful can say, "Oh yeah, I know *her*. My son used to play soccer with her kid."

That's who most of your friends are on Facebook.

To top it off, it *wasn't* her actual birthday!

Nobody is coming to your actual birthday party let alone your early birthday party!

You can thank random chance for the one person who showed! She was hungry, passed that restaurant on the way home, and found your stupid ass blubbering about the 575 no-shows!

Fucking Facebook

There is a whole group of people that like to check Facebook before they go to bed. I can understand checking on your kid before you go to sleep. But checking on Facebook? That is fucking pathetic. Here is an example of the corny bullshit these people post at night.

> 🐱 I'm about to have a threesome! Me, my bed, and my pillow! Goodnight Facebookers!

Yuck! How fucking cringe-worthy can you get?

An adult man wrote *I'm about to have a threesome! Me, my bed, and my pillow! Goodnight Facebookers!* Instead of trying to get a woman to have sex with him, this loser is fantasizing about fucking his bed and sharing his corny fantasy on Facebook. This post should really say I'm about to have a threesome! Me, my hand, and some gay porn!

Nobody Noticed

I'm sure you know people like this next woman. They have their smartphones set up so they are notified every time someone posts a comment on their page.

> 😃 I'm sorry I've been busy all day and didn't have time to check in, what did I miss?

There was one reply to this. Her friend wrote, *Well . . . Obama is still president. LOL!*

First, you don't have to say you are sorry. Nobody is looking for an apology. Nobody noticed you didn't check your news feed.

I looked at your page you have twenty-six friends. Those twenty-six people weren't talking about you all day. Nobody said, *Where the hell is she? What's going on with her?*

These kinds of conversations never happened. Nobody missed you. Nobody wondered what you are doing.

That didn't happen.

Why?

Because nobody cares!

If you want interesting news why are you checking Facebook?

Are you thinking, *I wonder if the guy I barely know that lives in Cincinnati is posting today about the local weather. I don't live there, never have, and have actually never been there before and it's the winter so I'm thinking it's probably cold but let me check his feed anyway because I missed important info because I was busy.*

But then again, what would Facebook be if people weren't afraid they will miss something important? You know what's important? *Your kids!* How about checking in with them five times per day to see how they're doing? They need some attention because they're being ignored by their parents who are distracted by their phones.

One Less Loser

> I woke up this morning with one less friend on Facebook. Did I make someone mad?

You did make someone mad. ME! A grown man posted this! Yes a man! Well with this kind of post he won't be a man for long as I'm sure he is in the process of transitioning into a woman.

Sir, did you ever consider that you have one less friend because that friend decided he doesn't want to be on Facebook?

Think about it. One of your more sane buddies woke up one morning and thought; *I'm forty-one years old. I have a hot wife. I have two great kids, and a good small circle of friends. My life is complete. I don't need this drama on Facebook. I don't want to worry about getting shit from some guy I hung out with twenty years ago for a couple of months, asking me why I didn't "like" his video of his dog fetching a stick.*

He didn't want to deal with some old friend sending him messages like:

Dude, we fucking hung that whole summer. We were pretty close. I posted that funny video of my dog and heard nothing from you. I know you have dogs, I figured you could relate.

That guy is trying to feed his two kids. He smartly decided that he doesn't want to be getting the kids ready for bed and have to deal with a Facebook message from an idiot.

Dude you have a dog I thought you could relate to my video!

Next time you play fetch with your dog throw the stick into traffic!

Officially No One Cares

Here's another idiot who believes Facebook friends are real friends who actually care about your life.

 Officially back on Facebook! Please everyone hold your applause!

Don't worry, sir. Nobody clapped. Nobody was excited that you reopened an account. Nobody even noticed you were gone. I'll hold my applause until you're back off of Facebook.

Goodnight Moron

Maybe you've read your kid the book *Goodnight Moon*. In the book, a little baby says goodnight to all the things in his room and the things he sees outside his window. Well, there seems to be a large amount of Facebook babies who love to do the same damn thing and it is one of the absolutely worst things I've ever read on the site.

 Goodnight Facebook!

Fuuuuuccckkk! I can read that post a hundred fucking times and it still makes me feel like maggots are crawling all over my skin. What are you expecting back?

Goodnight don't let the bed bugs bite!

Are you going to read me a story?

One woman posted this:

> My bed is calling my name so I'm ready to tuck under my blanket and get warm. Goodnight my dear Facebook and stay warm.

I highly doubt your bed called your name since that's never happened in the history of mankind. There is no such thing as a talking bed. If this woman's bed talked to her it would say, "Please lay off the desserts, you're suffocating me every night." If anyone you know, even a family member, writes *Goodnight Facebook,* please delete them as a friend. When they ask why you got rid of them say, "Because you said goodnight to an imaginary object!"

CHAPTER TWO

MY FIRST PRANK CALLS

By the time I made it to junior high school I was honing my prank call skills. I had a lot of time to do that because I was always grounded. I ended up locked in my room for hours on end. I was bored out of my mind and started making prank calls to pass the time.

I even recruited my good friend Tony and we would do prank calls together. Our very first prank happened when we met a pretty girl named Donna at school.

Donna had the biggest tits either of us had ever seen. Donna's rack was so powerful it inspired us to prank her. There was no planning or method to our madness, we searched the phonebook, found Donna's home phone number, and cold-called her.

"Hello," Donna said.

We froze. Snickered.

"Who is this?"

I launched into my first improvisation.

"Hello ma'am. We're doing a national survey; can we ask you a question? What is your bra size?"

"Who'd you say you were?" Donna demanded.

Donna was stacked, but she was also very smart! It didn't take her long to create a mental lineup of who might be calling.

"*Who* is this?" She asked again, this time with a knowing tone. She sounded like she knew it was Tony and I.

"Uh . . . never mind!"

We hung up immediately!

The next day in school Donna marched over to the two worst perverts in her class, the two boys that were always drooling over her tits, and doing very little to hide it.

"Hey Jim! Hey Tony!" She said mocking us. "Grow the *fuck* up!"

Before we could say a word, Donna walked out the door. Looking back, I think her bra size was a 34C. I know that because she had the same size rack as my grandmother.

MILP's: Mothers I'd Like to Prank

The Donna-Big-Tits call wasn't even close to successful, but it was the start of a career in making prank calls.

Tony and I graduated to calling random numbers. We would dial nonstop until we heard a distinctly feminine voice and pull our pranks. One time we were taking turns blurting out our nonsense and I saw a note on Tony's fridge. It was a phone number titled *Mom's Work Number*. So of course, I dialed it. It was Tony's turn to do the prank and I handed him the receiver and ran to the other phone to listen.

"Hello?"

"Hello ma'am . . . how big are your *tits*?" Tony asked.

There was a long, very awkward pause.

"*Tony*? Is that *you*?" His mother asked.

Tony was horrified and slammed the phone. He immediately figured out what I had done.

"YOU ASSHOLE!" he yelled and chased me through the house and around the neighborhood for the next half hour.

We've been friends ever since.

Awful Facebook Rule #2: Brag, Brag, Brag!

I can't think of anything more brutal than reading updates from people bragging about themselves.

Rule #2 for *How to Be Awful on Facebook* is all about the art of bragging. Facebook is filled with idiots declaring themselves smart and sexy. They post their horrible pictures, sit back, and wait for us to reply with our praise—these people epitomize what it means to be awful on Facebook. By the way, I will never use the horrific word *selfie* in this book. I'd rather get a blood transfusion from Magic Johnson.

In a nutshell if you are a bragger you want your friends to think you are wonderful while you make them feel like shit. You want everyone to believe you are living the life of your dreams but you aren't—your life is full of unhappiness. The bragging covers that up.

Bragging is a consequence of insecurity. This generation is obsessed with being validated. They grew up in homes where mom worked, dad worked, and nobody was around until the late evening. When the parents got home, you had dinner with them for forty-five minutes then everyone parted ways and didn't talk again until the next day at dinner. Mommy and Daddy didn't give them enough attention so they look for it online.

According to these braggers, they have ideal children, they are in perfect physical shape, eat healthy all the damn time, work longer hours, and are more productive than the rest of us. It's all smoke and mirrors designed to boost the bragger's ego and make the rest of us feel like shit.

How Not to Get Laid

What's amazing is how many guys are on Facebook bragging. They remind us how they are good looking. Most men know this turns a woman off but they keep posting. Take this fucking asshole as an example:

> 🐻 Ha, I remember growing up, my mother always told me that I could be anything I wanted to be when I became an adult. I'm thankful I chose to be sexy. LOL.

A grown man in his late thirties wrote this and posted it with a picture of himself at the gym.

Notice how he put a *Ha* and a *LOL* in there to soften it up. He's trying to say he's joking around. We all know he meant every word.

I bet he spent twenty minutes taking the right picture before he posted it. Plus, there is nothing funny about it. I'm still trying to figure out the joke?

If you wonder why the rest of the world hates Americans, this is it! I'm so disgusted after reading this post, I'm thinking about joining ISIS.

GAMBLERS NEVER WIN IN A CASINO

Recently I was in a third-rate casino in Vegas. When I'm in a place like that, I'm surrounded by misery.

The decor is horrible. The carpets look like shit. There are no clocks and no sunlight. All the dealers look like extras from *The Walking Dead* and nobody is having fun. Everybody is miserable.

The line to the ATM is out the door. People need more money because they keep losing. People are staring at slot machines chain-smoking cigarettes because they have to calm their nerves. They have to do that because they are dumping all their kid's college tuition money into a machine that's rigged by the casino. Now their kid can barely go to a community college because of their gambling habit.

They're not going to win. They never will. You hear some of these guys say, *but I was one more bar away from winning $10,000.* Guess what, the casino does that on purpose so people keep thinking they have a chance. Nobody has ever bought a house by playing cards in Vegas. Nobody has ever bought a brand-new Mercedes because they were playing craps. Give it up! It's not going to happen!

Mirror, Mirror, Who's the Biggest Douche?

This update is from a single guy. I should thank this douche. I'm back out on the dating scene and some nights I doubt myself. But, if this is my competition I'm going to clean up.

So earlier, I walked into the bathroom to wash my hands, prior to eating some lunch, and I see this beautiful picture hanging on the wall. I mean this was a truly mesmerizing picture! One might even say it was perfect. However, after about thirty seconds of eyeing this immaculate work of art, I then realized, Oh shit! That's just the mirror and this spectacular picture is indeed a picture of me! LOL!

That's what's out there, ladies! Narcissistic jerk-offs!

I have sixteen-year-old nieces that will text me sometimes and write LOL at the end.

I can accept that from a sixteen-year-old girl. It seems appropriate for her age. But not a grown man who writes long paragraphs about admiring himself in the mirror and ends it with *laughing out loud*!

I'm curious, how many women read this post and had the sudden urge to start eating pussy?

King Cock Sucker

> So I normally shave my head and line it up all sexy. To-night, I stepped up my game. I took off the sides and back giving myself a look fit for a king.

Nobody thinks you're sexy! Your head looks like a swollen ball sack.

That's good that you shaved your head. Now, the guy you're blowing will be able to hold on to your ears while he shoves his *fit-for-a-king* cock down your throat!

Dump This Dumpster Diver

It seems more acceptable for women to post a lot of pictures of them-selves but some women don't know when to stop. Take this stupid chick for instance. She wants everyone to tell her she is naturally pretty. To get compliments she posted a picture of herself dressed like a crack whore.

> I like the kind of guy who thinks you're beautiful with-out makeup on, when your hair is a mess, and you're in sweatpants and a T-shirt.

Good luck trying to find that type of guy. I'm really shocked that her relationship status says single. You know the only men that like that look? Homeless guys! Because they have the same outfit on! Strippers leaving the strip club after a night of dancing dress like that too on their way to their car. That's why you never hear about a strip-per getting raped in the parking lot. I saw one walking to her car that was giving me lap dances all night and I asked for my money back.

Magic Bragging

Talk about magical thinking—this woman takes positive affirmations to a new level of crazy!

> If you're reading this—I'm beautiful!

Really!? I read it and saw your profile pic and on a scale of 1–10 you are still a 4. If you lived in LA, you would be a *negative* 2. I hope you find someone out there who thinks you're beautiful. What about that mirror douche from a few paragraphs ago? He can stare at himself while he's fucking you.

Delusions of Grandeur

Here's a woman determined to let everyone know she's better than the rest of us.

> I have tattoos, piercings, and a Ph.D. I've dated rock stars and I'm a kick ass mom who bakes awesome cookies. I'm a badass piercer and I own my own home. I even have my own pet pig for that matter. I'm better than any basic bitch out there. I'm saying this because I need to remember these things. Yeah, I know you are looking at your wife or girlfriend right now and thinking, yeah, this chick is right she's a badass!

Piercings, tattoos, and dated rock stars? You sound more like a train wreck whore with Daddy issues. By the way, you didn't date any rock stars. That rock star did a show in your town, fucked you, and left. He did the same thing with another girl in the next town.

But hey, at least you can bake cookies. You have that going for you. Unfortunately, your cookies are not awesome. Your kid says that because kids love cookies. Try getting them on a shelf in a store if they are that damn good. You can't because they're mediocre just like your shitty tattoos.

Crazy-Baiter

Many of the bragging posts are of the bait-and-switch variety. For instance, this woman lists her shitty qualities and hits us with reverse psychology.

> ♥   I may be crazy, funny, random, and slightly insane but you've got to love me.

What she really means here is she's a drama queen and whenever she goes out with a group of people she causes a problem and ruins the night. Thank God for Uber now. You can throw this disaster of a human being in one and continue your night out. Then the next day she will ask you if you saw her phone because she lost it. Cunt.

Fitness Freaks

Fitness freaks are some of the worst braggers on Facebook. These assholes brag about being in shape and clutter our news feed with pictures showing off their bodies and workout clothes. They can't wait to make their friends feel like shit.

> 💪   If I lift up my arms any further, my biceps are going to explode. The pump is real!

No, person's bicep has ever exploded, asshole.

The pump is real?

What pump? The one you have to use to get your dick hard for women because you're so in love with yourself? Why don't you do everyone a favor and pump yourself up with a lethal dose of heroin!

Cumshake Regrets

> 🏋 I may feel exhausted, weak and sometimes nauseous after my workout, but one thing I never feel is regret.

Why would you feel *regret* after working out? Did you cheat on your wife by blowing the trainer in the locker room? Do you regret he didn't kiss you after you gave him oral?

That is the only reason you should feel regret after a workout!

When you exercise and lift weights, you're doing something good and healthy for yourself. No one gets distraught after a good workout, goes home, and drinks himself to sleep.

We know what this guy is doing; it's another case of backdoor bragging. He wants to be complimented.

Yea! You went to the gym! Good for you dude, none of us are impressed.

Wait, what's this? *You feel nauseous?*

Who the fuck feels nauseous after a workout?

Maybe your stomach hurts because of that cum milkshake you had in the gym locker room?

Well, at least you got your protein for the day. Did you ask him if his cum was GMO free?

The Gym Whore

Here's another idiot looking for a backdoor compliment.

> 😊 Me and the gym have been in a steady relationship for a while now and I couldn't be happier. Even though I have to share her with other people I know, I have a special place in her heart.

Guess what—everybody else in your neighborhood is fucking her too! Just think of all those slimeballs grunting, pumping their hard iron inside her, sweating while they do it, wiping off with a nasty towel, and then taking off. This goes on all day and all night. I hope your gym breaks your heart by going out of business. Next time I drive by your gym, I'll make sure I stop in and take a shit!

Running on Empty

People love to brag about running charity races. Who the fuck cares? Is there anybody in the history of running 5K's that hasn't posted their participation on Facebook? They get to brag two times. I can do charity work and exercise at the same time. *Look how fucking awesome I am!* I'm sure you've seen the following post.

> 🙂 Just ran a 5K!

Great, you get a free T-shirt at the finish line that's way too big and you'll never wear. Let me guess, the charity is breast cancer awareness? Is there anyone on this planet that's not aware that women can get breast cancer? Thanks for reminding me. Now, let me check your tit for a lump!

> 😆 Just finished a 20-mile run after spin class!

No you didn't you fucking liar.

> So excited for the treadmill, my baby just bought me running shoes! I love that man!

He bought you running shoes because you're out of shape. If you were in shape, he would have bought you an easy chair.

> Running 17 miles on a treadmill is so boring!

I saw your profile picture dude. It looks like you did seventeen miles a day circling a buffet.

> About to meet my personal trainer. I made the first appointment.

Really? Wow! That is fucking *amazing*! You've paid someone $60 per hour to make you work out and you showed up? *You are an amazing person!* I see you're a hot chick, too, so I'm thinking the over-under for when you start fucking your trainer is three months.

Club Jerk-Off

A douchey gym guy posted this one.

> Going to Club Gym on this Friday night!

He should have just written, *No one wants to hang out with me tonight so I might as well go to the gym.*

Marathon Moaner

Even when these fitness freaks aren't working out, they find a way to brag about being athletic. Here's a woman that's running away from running and wants our sympathy.

> It breaks my heart to share that I won't be running the marathon in December due to a pulled muscle in my leg.

Then don't share it.

Keep it to yourself.

If you didn't share it maybe your heart wouldn't be broken. Out of your 459 friends, I bet only two remembered that you were running in a marathon.

Nobody gives a fuck you pulled a muscle. If your dog dies, then I'll feel bad for you. Pulling a muscle is not a crisis. There are marathons every two weeks. Just run in the next one, attention whore.

Handstand Hysteria

Here is another secret braggart who deserves zero encouragement!

> I'm not going to lie. I've been discouraged with my fitness journey the last couple of weeks. It's hard and every life challenge has come my way but just like having faith, I have continued to push through all the emotions and pain. And what do you know? I accomplished my first handstand in the process . . . then I accomplished the double under on the jump ropes. What? How did this happen? Patience and consistency. The small victories are what are keeping me going.

You know what takes patience? Reading that horseshit you wrote. She starts off, *I'm not going to lie.*

No one asked you if you were lying. Are you known as a liar? Even if you did, no one would be disappointed because no one gives a fuck!

I've been discouraged with my fitness journey, she says.

You go to the gym a few days a week and exercise. You're *not* on a journey. The gym is a mile from your house. You go there, lift weights, and do cardio for thirty minutes and leave. None of those activities are remotely close to a journey.

It's hard and every life challenge has come my way.

You're squatting eight-pound pink dumbbells. How is that a life challenge?

I have continued to push through all the emotions and pain.

What emotions do you have in the gym? Are you really crying? I've never seen someone running on a treadmill and bawling her eyes out.

You're a drama queen. No wonder you're making a big deal about working out.

This woman is thirty-seven years old, and she's bragging about doing a handstand and jumping rope. My five-year-old niece does those things everyday and never says a word. If anyone should brag, it's the five-year-old. I'm not impressed by your handstand. I'm more impressed by the wall holding up your lard ass!

Workout Withdrawals

> 🙁 I haven't been to the gym in a few days. I'm having withdrawals.

No, you're not. You're not shaking in a corner. You don't need the emergency room.

No one is walking by you with concern, *Holy shit look at that guy. He must have withdrawals from not going to the gym.* I'll believe it if you tell me people keep asking you if you have Parkinson's.

Cheat-Day Cunts

Another form of fitness bragging is the *diet brag*. People post pictures of the healthy food they are eating or they complain about their diet. Ironically, most of the pictures are updates about the dieter's *cheat day*. This is a fitness buzzword for the day you eat anything you want. Read the next post, you'll see there is nothing worse than a guy bragging about his diet.

> I usually eat clean but for some reason, we just decided to grill rib eyes and have oversized baked potatoes last night. I guess that was my cheat day for the week!

Wow, you are wonderful! How can I have willpower like you?

You ate an oversized baked potato and steak and you consider that a cheat day? If it's a cheat day, how about you let me fuck your girlfriend? You can eat your oversized potato and I'll stick my dick in your girlfriend's oversized snatch!

Here's another fitness fuck-head on the same wavelength. It's a woman bragging about a diet she's not following.

> I'm offered a cheat day diet wise, but today's choice may not have been the best idea. Can somebody say, "I'll be paying for this for a couple of days?" Holy salt intake!

Holy salt intake?

First, fuck you and your cheat day.

Second, nobody gives a shit unless the salt intake came from your husband. Did you finally swallow his load? Well, congratulations to him. Maybe every day will be a cheat day in your marriage? Well, until you start looking good and decide to fuck your personal trainer.

GARY FROM FLORIDA:
MEGATOR THE BONECRUSHER

I've known Gary from Florida for over thirty years. The most important weapon in his sexual arsenal is his confidence. Sometimes during my podcast, I play the devil's advocate and question his tactics or motives but it doesn't faze him. He's polite with his responses and even thoughtful but nothing puts a dent in his brashness. He knows what he wants and goes after it. As he says, *I'm a first-ballot hall of famer, fella!*

His confidence is most apparent when he talks about his dick. *Megator the Bonecrusher,* he says proudly, *that's the name of my mule!* Gary doesn't get into the mental trap of worrying about dick size. *Back in the day Megator the Bonecrusher was a good 8 and 1/8th,* he says. *Now that I'm older and it's shrunk I think it's closer to 6 and 1/16th. So, sometimes I call it Mini-Meg! But look fella, Ron Jeremy, that fat fuck, doesn't have nothing on me!* Gary's lesson is clear: *It doesn't matter the size, it matters what you do with the equipment.*

Gary only dates women that show love for Megator. *If a woman doesn't want to suck my mule, I move on, that's a relationship killer, a true deal breaker!* Gary believes dick pride builds sexual confidence and sexual confidence leads to better sex. *Hair is out. I shave down there. I look like a fucking eight-year-old and women love it!* Nothing should get in the way of worshiping the moose knuckle. *I don't even cover it with a bag, it just gets in the way!* That's Gary's rule about sexual confidence: honor your cock and it will work hard to make you proud every time!

Super Shitheads

Bragging about doing chores is another type of Facebook bragging that needs to stop. There is nothing amazing about doing work you are required to do. These next few posts are from people that don't understand that. They think they are *superheroes*.

> 🚀 Today's agenda requires super powers. Has anybody seen my cape?

Nope, I didn't see a cape!

I saw your profile picture and you really don't need a cape. You need a black dress, pointy black hat, and a broom.

> 🌵 If I had a superpower I wouldn't use it to cure cancer or stop ISIS, I'd hem my pants!

You would never have a superpower because there is no such thing. When a superhero movie starts, it never says it's based on a true story. There is no such thing as superheroes! But, I could be wrong because I thought there was no such thing as a grown man that likes to hem his pants.

> 🌲 I'm in such a cleaning mood today, LOL!

Who laughed at that? What is funny about being in a *cleaning mood*? There isn't an ounce of humor in that statement. The best comedic actor couldn't make this post funny.

When people put *laughing out loud* in their own posts, it's like they are in a bad sitcom. They crack a corny joke and then insert the laugh track ... *lolololololololol*!

This is like telling your friends—smile here! Laugh here! Let your friends laugh when they want to fucking laugh. They don't need your direction.

If you are in such a cleaning mood, clean up your shitty Facebook updates that are cluttering my news feed, jerk-off!

Gourmet Gross-out

> I made a delicious beef stew with my new Crock-Pot, then saw a preview for Horrible Bosses 2. Get this day some butter, it's on a roll.

You might think that your beef stew is delicious but nobody else does. There are seventy-five different chef shows on TV and you're not on any of them. There's a reason you're not a fucking chef in a restaurant. You make stew by pouring it out of a can. It's not delicious.

Try putting that in a real restaurant and see if people will order it. Your family or friends might tell you it looks good because they don't want to hurt your feelings. It looks like a bowl of shit and nobody wants to see a fucking picture of that.

Get this day some butter, it's on a roll? Are you fucking kidding me? That could be the worst thing I've ever read in my life. I'd rather read a post that says I've been charged with kiddie porn.

> Cooked shrimp alfredo! LOL! Jealous?

Cooking shrimp alfredo is not the feat of a genius chef.

Cooking from a recipe is like a garage band doing cover songs in a shitty bar. It's me going on stage and telling George Carlin jokes.

Likewise, it takes zero brainpower to follow directions on a box of shrimp alfredo. A trained monkey can stir that shit until it's heated. Nobody is impressed.

If you have a shellfish allergy and end up choking on that plate of pasta that would be funny. I'd laugh at that—*lolololol*!

Porky's Roll

Assholes that brag about finishing work early are the worst. *Brutal!* Why do we care? We don't but that doesn't stop people like this teacher.

> 🧑 I just finished grading my tests! Call me a pork roll with egg and cheese cuz I'm on a roll.

I've come across a lot of these that say, *I'm on a roll.*

This woman gives it a new twist. I don't know what a pork roll with egg and cheese is, but it sounds fucking horrible.

When you write this shit, you're telling your Facebook friends you did the work you're supposed to do. *Aren't you fucking impressive!*

This woman is a teacher. Their job is not harder than others. She gives tests, takes them home, grades them, and then brings them back the next day.

I'll like your post if you write, "Just fucked 4 students in the last month! Call me a pork roll with egg and cheese cuz I'm on a roll."

Compliment Bait

Bragging about your children or spouse is another shitty way people get validation online. People who do this are using their loved ones as compliment bait. For example, this next post is from a woman who doesn't really care what people think about her kid, she's jealous and wants to turn the spotlight back on herself.

> Cooper is such a cutie. He's already getting all the attention.

Guess what, the kid gets attention because he's three years old. People naturally respond to little kids in a positive way.

When I walk in a room and I see a little kid, I'll go right over to him. Most of the time my other options are people who are standing around, staring into their phones, gossiping, and talking about a new iPhone app.

Kids are interesting but you're not. That's why he is getting all the attention, you fucking dummy. When you spread your legs that fateful night, you should have known the days of it being about *you* were over!

Sounds of Stupid

> Whenever I say the word "cow" my baby makes noises. She's only one! #SmartOneYearOld #SmartCookie

Every one-year-old child makes noises you dumb fuck. And what the fuck is a smart cookie? Is that a term they use on that nerd show *Big Bang Theory* that I've never watched because I don't have conversations on who would win in a fight, Batman or Superman?

On second thought, maybe I'm wrong. The kid could be a genius. Let's test that.

Have her do your taxes this year. Let's see how that works out for you. Let's see if the IRS has an issue with forms being filled out in crayon.

Complete & Utter Horseshit

This next parent posted a Facebook brag that is super cringe-worthy.

> Tonight, I come to you with complete and utter honesty. My wee one was so completely amazing today, she is such an inspiration, I can only hope she stays on this path. Let's all have faith that I can continue to be that parent she needs because after all that's where it all begins. Thank you for this amazing child that calls me Mom!

Brag, brag, brag!

Let's all have faith? Why?

Faith has nothing to do with taking care of your child. Just make good decisions and everything will be fine. If you've been drinking, don't drive. If the kid is in the car, don't text. Most of parenting is based on common sense. You don't need your friends' prayers to figure out what to do. The only time I ask my friends for prayers is if the condom breaks with some chick I met off of Tinder.

Looney Tunes Loser

> Disney songs! Drinking! Still up! Winning! Party until tomorrow! YOLO!

This loser posted this with a picture of playing cards and some beer bottles. Okay, that's normal. But, who in the fuck listens to Disney songs when they are playing poker? That has to be one of the worst fucking nights a guy could imagine. You need to focus when playing cards. When I think of Disney I think of overcrowding, kids crying, and fat people in my way.

Four years ago, I played cards with some guys at a friend's house. The homeowner was super drunk and losing all his money. After losing his last hand, he jumped on the table, pulled his pants down, and took a shit all over the table. That's how you play cards with your friends.

CHAPTER THREE

CONSTRUCTION STORIES

Making crank calls and pulling pranks on your friends is age appropriate when you are in junior high. All young boys have a phase where they are crazy and immature but most kids eventually outgrow it. I never did. My pranks seemed to get more awful and more disgusting the older I got.

Some of my worst years were between the ages of twenty and twenty-four. During that time, I had zero direction in life and lost my way. I became a disgusting slob and lived like a fucking animal.

My dream of becoming a comedian was on the shelf. So far back on the shelf, I lost all sight of it. My brothers worked in real estate and bought old shitty houses to flip and resell. Luckily, they found out I needed a job and took pity on me.

There were a few good things about working construction. I could zone out while I was ripping sheetrock off the walls and picking up trash. Also, some of my good friends worked with me. That meant I could play jokes on them when I was miserable and bored.

Piss Cubes

One miserable summer I was working with my friend Vinnie and we were helping my brother Joe demolish the inside of an old house.

The house had been abandoned for some time. The air conditioner was broken. Clothes and trash were up to our ankles. Cat shit littered the house like little landmines. The place was disgusting, dirty, and about 100 degrees inside. It was a fucking hellhole!

The first day we worked there was a complete disaster with garbage littered all over the place. The only good thing in the whole damn place was a refrigerator. For some reason, it still worked. I took note it had a small freezer inside.

One day I went to get a drink and found two empty ice cube trays in the freezer. When no one was looking, I took the trays into the bathroom and took a piss in them. I made sure every single one of the twenty-four squares was filled perfectly. I put them back in the freezer and told no one about it. To this day, I don't know what possessed me to do that.

Cut to a week later, someone bought sandwiches at the local deli and the crew sat down to eat lunch in the kitchen. I noticed my buddy Vinnie was drinking lemonade out of a glass jar. The sound of his ice clinking around in the jar was like an alarm going off.

"Vinnie, where'd you get the ice?!"

"From the freezer."

"Oh, really?"

"Yeah, there was an ice cube tray in there and figured I use the ice."

Holy fuck, he's drinking my piss cubes!

Adrenaline pulsed through my body when I realized what was happening. I'm older than Vinnie but he's pushing 6'2" and weighs in at 240. He's my friend but he could easily kick my ass.

On this day, Vinnie wasn't in the mood to fuck around. He was hot and he'd worked hard all day so I was scared as shit to tell him about the piss cubes because I knew it would send him over the edge and he would murder me. So, I waited.

In fact, I waited exactly fifteen years. By that time, Vinnie was married and had five kids. I had a gig in New Jersey at the Stress

Factory and it happened to be on his birthday so I invited him, his family, and friends to the club.

When the show started, Vinnie was seated at a large reserved table in the back of the room. The room was packed. There were about 350 people there and Vinnie had another twenty people at his table celebrating with him. Everyone was laughing and having fun.

About midway through my set, I told the audience, "Hey everyone, my friend Vinnie is here tonight. He's celebrating his birthday. Give him a big round of applause!"

Then, I launched into the piss cubes story. I explained it in great detail right up to that moment when I watched him suck down those pieces of golden-colored ice. The crowd went fucking crazy.

I yelled out to Vinnie, "How does feel to know you drank my piss, Vinnie?"

Even though he was all the way in the back, I could hear him screaming like a crazy man.

"Fuck you! Fuck you motherfucker! You're fucking dead after the show!"

The whole audience was laughing hysterically.

Later, Vinnie said, "I really wanted to get up and fucking kill you! Why didn't you tell me those ice cubes were piss?" I said, "What fun would that be? By the way, Happy Birthday!"

Shit Bag Surprise

I played another prank on Vinnie while we were working in that same house. The bathroom was especially disgusting. The floor and the tub were overflowing with trash. Vinnie was asked to paint the ceiling before he cleaned it out so if the paint dripped down it wouldn't hurt anything.

It was ninety degrees outside. We were all sweating our asses off but it was worse for Vinnie because he was crammed in that little bathroom and it felt like an oven. Vinnie would take frequent smoke breaks to get out of the heat. One time while he was out, I went in the bathroom, took a shit in a brown grocery bag, and hid the bag underneath all the trash. I told the other guys what I did and ran back upstairs to my job.

Vinnie comes back in to finish his painting and immediately screams.

"WHAT THE FUCK! IT FUCKING STINKS IN HERE! DID SOMEONE TAKE A SHIT IN HERE? WHAT THE HELL IS GOING ON?"

Everyone ran to the bathroom.

"What are you talking about Vinnie?" I asked.

"Don't you smell this? It wasn't like this before. It fucking stinks!" He was livid.

All the guys denied smelling the shit bag. "No, man. We don't smell anything."

"YOU DON'T SMELL IT?" He yelled.

"Nope. Don't smell a thing!" I said.

"I can't stand this. This is fucking horrible."

The whole day Vinnie worked with that bag of shit right next to him. Every hour he'd lose his patience and erupt!

"MOTHERFUCKER!"

I'd yell down, "What happened? Did you spill the paint?"

"Man, this is driving me crazy. It smells like someone took a shit right under my nose."

I would come down, pretend to look for the bag, and go through the same routine. "Vin let me check this again. I don't smell anything. Where is it coming from?"

"How can you not smell that?"

This went on for the whole fucking day. Right before we quit, he started throwing everything out of the room because he couldn't take it anymore and he finally found the bag. He went fucking crazy and yelled.

"WHO THE FUCK DID THIS?!"

There was no hiding this one. I had the biggest smirk on my face and couldn't stop laughing. He figured out it was me. Then, he whipped the shit bag across the room and hit me right in the chest with it. The prank was well worth getting hit by a shit bag.

Morning Traffic Turds

Part of this time, I lived in Florida with my friend Dave. Dave and I would work as laborers on the local construction sites. We would grind it out for a week, get the paycheck, then quit, and live off the money for another few weeks.

One of these construction jobs was on the corner of a busy intersection. They were building a massive condominium complex and while they cleared the field they put a Porta-John on the edge of the site. It ended up twenty feet from the main traffic signal. If you opened the door, you were staring right at people waiting for the light to change.

The second day on the job, I climbed in the Porta-John and took a shit while Dave held the door open. He pretended that he was fixing the hinges while I dropped a deuce. It was nine o'clock in the morning. Rush hour traffic was crawling by and my stunt became the main attraction. People were honking, yelling, and screaming at me.

"SHUT THAT DAMN DOOR!"

"THAT IS DISGUSTING YOU FUCKING IDIOT!"

The beeping and honking was insane and I sat there with a straight face reading the paper with my pants down to my ankles. Someone must have complained because the next day the Porta-John was turned around and facing the construction site.

MORE ANNOYING AIRPLANE ANNOUNCEMENTS

A while back, I took a red-eye flight. The plane was late and we were stuck at the gate for hours. Everyone was sitting in those black leather metal armchairs. Airports call them *passenger terminal chairs*. They have zero padding and make your ass numb in two minutes. You can't recline or take a nap in them. They might as well be concrete benches.

The gate attendant keeps updating us saying, "Please remain comfortably seated." That's impossible! No one is comfortable in these fucking seats! I've never been in someone's house that has these chairs. Can you imagine that?

"Are those the seats from the airport?"

"Yeah, they are so damn comfortable we had to get them for our house."

That has never happened because they are horrible. They stink!

We get on the plane and we are delayed again. We sat on the runway for two hours. Everybody is sleeping because it is one o'clock in the morning. Then, they make announcements on how to put a seat belt on. Everybody knows how to put a fucking seat belt on. My five-year-old son knows how to put a seat belt on. You click it in and then you click it out.

Next, they start in on the carry-on bags. "Make sure you are careful when you open the overhead compartment. The bags may have shifted during the flight."

Those bags never shift! Everything is stuffed in there so tight I need a hammer and a chisel just to get my bags out. If the plane flew upside down and you opened that compartment, none of the bags would shift.

Then, they tell us about the drink cart. Everybody is sleeping but they announce it anyway, "The drink cart is coming around. We have Coke, Diet Coke, Mountain Dew, orange juice, Coors, Coors Light."

We fucking know! Just say the drink cart is on its way! I feel everyone knows what's on the cart. It'll be soda and beer. Do you have to name ninety different things? How about when you pull up everybody looks at the selection?

Last but not least, they remind us three times that there is no smoking on the flight. There hasn't been smoking on a flight since 1995! You can't even smoke outside anymore. Why would you be able to smoke on a plane? Where is the ashtray on the plane? Do they think we expect the flight attendant to take our cigarette butts when we are done smoking? After they make that announcement, to the next flight attendant I see I say, "Excuse me but did they say smoking or nonsmoking on this flight?" The dirty look I get is precious.

Awful Facebook Rule #3: Motivate People with Your Bullshit!

Reading motivational Facebook posts is the worst! It's ironic how a few sentences meant to inspire you can instead make you want to slit your wrists. That's the exact feeling I have every time I read someone posting their inspirational horseshit online.

This makes coming up with the third rule of *How to Be Awful on Facebook* very easy—*motivate people with your bullshit!*

These kinds of posts are usually just shitty retreads of Oprah-wisdom. They stink! You can get better inspiration out of a fortune cookie. Nothing says I'm a loser more than posting a quote about being a winner.

Think Positive!

There are a few types of motivational advice that reoccur on Facebook: think positive, have no regrets, accept yourself, be tough, set goals, and take action.

Think positive is a self-help phrase that has been run into the ground. It's impossible to think positive all the damn time. I'll think positive next time someone I don't like is waiting for their AIDS results. Check this horrific post out.

I'm Positive This Is Bullshit

Here's this woman's update:

> Health is not just about what you're eating, it's also about what you're thinking!

Okay lady, so you're telling us that health is linked to what you're eating and what you're *thinking*? Are you trying to say positive thinking is good for you? *Get the fuck out of here!*

Just one question, how would it affect your health if you ate my sweaty ass? What? You're not sure if you'd like it? Just think positive thoughts and I'm sure it will be a great experience for you!

Happiness Is Not a Choice, Cunt!

I'm sure you know assholes like this next woman. Don't you hate it when a person has a run of good luck and suddenly becomes an expert on how to live? This is exactly what this awful Facebook hag is doing:

> Happiness is a choice. However, nothing is free. So if you want to be happy, work hard. Do good. Plan ahead. And overcome the obstacles with a smile and awareness you can achieve whatever your heart desires! #nolimits #happiness #smile #beauty #goals

Hashtag—YUCK! This is a cringe-worthy string of clichés. Let's break down this cunt's fucked-up philosophy. First, she writes:

Happiness is a choice!

No, happiness is not a choice! There are a lot of mentally ill people out there that feel sad. They don't want to feel sad but they have no choice. They were born with this problem. There is something wrong with their brain. They want to feel happiness but they can't. So happiness is *not* a choice. Right off the bat you're fucking wrong!

However, nothing is free.

Once again, this isn't true! There's a lot of free shit out there. Go to Costco on Saturday. Walk through the store and you'll find free samples every three feet. Go run in a charity race and they'll give you a free water bottle and a shitty T-shirt. Check into a Double-Tree hotel and they give you a free cookie that I always turn down by saying I'm not five years old anymore!

So if you want to be happy, work hard.

I know many people who are retired. They stopped working *hard* a long time ago and they are very happy about it! I know people that don't work hard and they are just as happy.

Most people who work hard are *not happy* because they are so focused on their work. They work so fucking much that they don't have time to be happy! So that proves there's another thing wrong with your goofy inspirational post.

Do good. Plan ahead.

Really? Is that how you become happy? You *plan ahead*? How does that make anyone happy? Planning ahead just means you're organized. I know a lot of people that don't plan ahead and are disorganized and are very happy so once again this woman is wrong.

And overcome the obstacles with a smile and awareness you can achieve whatever your heart desires! #nolimits

Yes, there are limits!

I want to be the lead singer of AC/DC but that will not happen!

Why can't I be the lead singer? Because someone already has that job. Also, I can't sing and I have no fucking ear for music. Even if they needed a new lead singer, they wouldn't let me. That limit proves I can't achieve *whatever my heart desires*!

Sometimes you're not good enough to achieve your heart's desire. It has nothing to do with *smiling* or *awareness*. If you aren't good at it, you aren't getting the fucking gig. I've had some obstacles in my life, I remember smiling at times when I was going through it, and when I woke up the next day the obstacles were still there. I don't know why they just didn't go away. I had awareness of the situation and I smiled. *Oh, I know why!* Because it didn't matter that I had both those things, I had to wait it out and when enough time passed I overcame the obstacle. So, fuck you and your dumb hashtags!

No Regrets!

No regrets is another motivational phrase that people love to post online.

It's in fashion to say you have *no regrets* but every human on earth has at least one thing they would do differently in their life. You may not dwell on it but you have regrets.

For instance, if you've ever wasted an hour on Facebook you have fucking regrets. In fact, I bet every person who knows this next guy regrets accepting him as a Facebook friend.

Bring the Bullshit

This guy's update epitomizes the no-regrets mentality:

> Having no regrets. I'm ready to show and prove to people that I'm ready for what lies ahead. So, bring it on!

Wow! Watch out everyone! This guy means business. No one should mess with this guy. He has *no regrets,* and he's *ready to show people he can handle what's ahead.* I'm fucking inspired and so are his friends. They wrote comments like:

Good for you, dude!

You're the man!

You can do it!

Wow, real clever comments.

What're you trying to prove, motherfucker? What lies ahead? Who are you talking to when you say *bring it on*? Bring what on? Are you being fucked in the ass later? Is that it? Then my comment would be:

Make sure the guy wears a bag!

The bottom line is this—anyone that says they have no regrets— has regrets!

That's my dumb meme! Feel free to copy this and spread it around the Internet.

No regrets? Yes, you have regrets. Your friends have regrets and I have regrets. The main regret is that I spent all this time reading your dumb fucking post.

GARY FROM FLORIDA: LOOK AT ME, FELLA!

If you want to study a man with cool self-confidence then Gary from Florida is your guy. When it comes to seducing women, he's at the top of his game. James Bond has nothing on Gary from Florida.

Perhaps you've heard the story about my last Waffle House visit with Gary. He had the name and phone number of the waitress before she took our order. Now, that may not seem like the biggest achievement since most Waffle House waitresses rank about a four on a good day, but it's not the quality of his conquests that matters, it's the *quantity*! Gary has professional-level stats when it comes to scoring with women.

Look at me, fella! That's his catchphrase and it suits him. He's like MacGyver, who can turn a paper clip into a weapon. Gary from Florida turns any situation into an effective moment of pussy wrangling.

If you are a man (or woman for that matter) who lacks confidence, you need to take a page from Gary's book. For instance, Gary has had many one-night stands. On occasion, some of these women, whom he really had a good time with, didn't text or call him back. Most guys would let that affect their ego and it would zap them of their self-confidence. Gary says, *The first thought that comes in your head shouldn't be "oh, man she didn't like me," it should be, "she couldn't take my mule! It was too damn much for her!"*

Sad, pathetic thinking only slows you down, *Yeah, you may have a little melancholy for a few days, but move on fella!* If you see her on the dating website flirting with other men, *Block the bitch and move on. There's plenty of fish in the sea, fella!*

If a woman doesn't go after my dick like she's going after that last tasty piece of steak meat with her fork and knife, then she ain't for me! That is the level of devotion Gary expects from women he dates. He shows the same level of dedication when he's eating their box so it better be mutual. He told a story about going down on a woman and she was a squirter. He said, *It felt like I was getting my teeth power washed fella!"*

Accept Yourself!

I think it may be a requirement for women who live on Facebook to post a weekly picture of themselves and write a lame caption about acceptance. *Accept yourself*—one of the other self-help clichés.

How about you post your affirmations on a mirror in your house and not on Facebook. Nobody cares!

The next woman can't help herself. She wants the whole world to think she's amazing!

Time for New Parts

This is a great example of a fucked-up philosopher who pretends to be making a statement of personal empowerment but is really fishing for compliments. It's her birthday, and she posts a picture of herself to show her friends what she looks like—warts and all.

She's staring in the mirror. No real expression, no makeup, and she's dressed down. She added this *inspiring* caption:

> This is what 36-years-old looks like on me. Always exhausted. Slightly overweight. Don't know how to smile seriously. Mother of two kids. Wife of 14 years. Still trying to figure it all out. Love to laugh. Day-dreamer. Happy to drink wine any day I want to and positively happy. Or, at least I try everyday to be. That's me! #HappyBirthday #MadeIn1979AllOriginalParts

Here is what I want to say to this woman. First, why don't you leave the taking pictures of yourself to your teenage daughter? You're almost forty. Point that camera at something more interesting like your thirty-six-year-old tits.

Second, it's crazy you like to drink wine! Fuck, I've never heard that. I don't know where I've been. When did middle-aged white women start drinking wine?

So, you don't know how to smile? You say you're slightly overweight. You're suffering because you are exhausted all the time. These things could be a problem. Is it possible you are having these issues because you are drunk all the time? All that wine you drink is just empty calories and is loaded with sugar and alcohol messes with your sleep pattern. There you go, I've known you one minute and I know why you're having all these problems.

Let's do a reality check. You look hot for thirty-six. You're not overweight. You look good for having two kids—a solid 7.5. I'll give you that. Also, you've been married for fourteen years and have two kids. That's good and deserves some respect.

In fact, you might be an inspiration to younger women. But, here's the thing, you already knew that! Be honest, lady. You wouldn't have posted this picture if you looked like shit. You posted this picture because you want everyone else to acknowledge you. You may think this is promoting self-acceptance, but it's just self-promotion. You are baiting everyone to get positive comments, like this:

OMG, there is nothing wrong with you!

You look amazing!

I hope I look like that at thirty-six.

You look like you are in your twenties!

You look ten years younger!

Here is some life advice. Get sober. Lose weight. Smile for a fucking change! And, replace one *original part* for me—that part of your brain that makes you post corny life lessons and shitty hashtags!

Pinnacle of Pathetic

Here is one of the most pathetic motivational posts I've ever read:

> My fault is that I don't realize how great I am. One day, I hope I can!

You think this chick is a little full of herself? What makes this post interesting is the first comment posted by one of her male friends. He wrote:

I don't get it? Why do you have to post this on Facebook and not to yourself in private?

This is fucking beautiful! *He called her out on her bullshit.*

After he made that comment nobody else responded. She was waiting for a comment about how great she was and it never came. Sounds like the people that know her know she has way more faults than just not knowing how great she is.

Not Winning

Here is a guy that has the *no regrets* mentality. Read how it worked out for him:

> I am the champion again in fantasy football! Revenge against my mother for defeating me last year. Oh, how sweet it is to win five titles in six years! I guess I'm the New England Patriots of a fantasy football league.

No, you're not the *New England Patriots of your fantasy football league.* You're just the *gay guy*! That's right, did you ever hear a conversation between two guys talking about fantasy football? The only time two guys stop babbling about fantasy football is when they're 69-ing each other.

Get Tough!

Get tough is another common philosophy on Facebook. Ironically, tough people are not on Facebook talking tough. But, it doesn't stop these pussies from spreading their cringe-worthy advice about how to handle the difficulties in our lives.

If I Ran for President

Here's a badass that wants to *get tough* on Congress:

> If I ran for president as an independent would you vote for me? Our platform would start with: Cut the crap Congress! Forget partisan politics! Do what's best for our people! Tell all the truth all the time! The buck stops here!

This guy must be on to something because no politician has ever thought of running on that platform. I think this guy can win with his fresh ideas.

I'll vote for you, sir. I'll vote for you to delete your Facebook page.

Punching the Clock

There are a lot of tough guys on Facebook. This guy might be one of the toughest! He's feeling *determined,* and he wants everyone to know it!

First, he does something that proves he's a manly man. When he gets to his dentist appointment, he checks in on his Facebook map. Did he think any of his friends were going to be hanging in the waiting room when he was done? Even if his best friend drove right by the place with plenty of time to kill, he wouldn't stop in. Who gives a fuck that you're at the dentist and nobody gives a shit that you're getting a root canal.

> Emergency root canal? Bring it! Not covered on the probationary period of new dental insurance? Come on 2016, is that all you've got? You punch like a girl!

Ooooooh! Don't mess this guy.

Look how he's calling out the year 2016!

This guy is scary!

I'm telling everyone, this motherfucker is *determined.*

Come on 2016, is that all you've got?

If 2016 could really talk back, he might say:

Yeah, unfortunately that's all I got. I'm sorry I punch like a girl. You got me, man! You're lucky your tooth didn't start acting up in 2015 because that year was an MMA fighter and he definitely didn't punch like a girl. I hear 2017 is going to be a pro football player so you better get all your teeth fixed this year because I'm basically a pussy. And by the way if you were such a tough motherfucker you claim to be you would wait to get the root canal until your new insurance kicks in.

Like My Tears? I'll Kill You!

This Facebook update is scary, sad, and pathetic. This guy has taken a picture of himself with his hand on his forehead and he has tears running down his face. Basically, he took a picture of himself while he was crying. Then, in the middle of his breakdown he wrote:

> Don't let the tears fool you. I will still knock the fuck out of someone!

What do you think is going on in this guy's mind at that moment? Just imagine yourself being this distraught. You're going through something horrible and you are crying about the situation. Then, you have the impulse to take a picture of yourself. You do this in the middle of your breakdown. How is that possible?

He's trying to send a message to his friends: *I'm sensitive but watch out, I can still beat your ass!*

This bizarre post got about thirty comments. They're things like:

Dude, everything okay?

You all right, man?

I got your back, bro.

All of the other comments are similar.

Do you think this guy might need attention?

How many pictures did he take to get the right one? Imagine him saying, *Nope, not enough tears in this one. I don't like this one either because my hair is a little messy and I want my hair to look good even though I'm sobbing like I lost my whole family in a car wreck.*

Fantasy Champion

It doesn't surprise me that a lot of *get tough* posts are from guys bragging about being great at sports. However, there are more posts about dudes bragging about *fantasy football.*

Imagine you are a grown man. You are on Facebook and posting about how good you are at *fantasy* football.

Let that sink in for a second. You're a forty-year-old man writing this shit:

> Fantasy football! I've been running my own league since 1992 when we scored out of the morning paper. Since then, after all these years, and playing in multiple leagues on some years, but usually played in just one league. I estimate that I have played in 45 leagues.

This is the nerd's version of playing golf or Dungeons and Dragons. Guys that don't want to be around their wives play fantasy football. So, they waste all their fucking time with this nonsense.

> I've won all three this year! I crushed it! I think I have won 13 of 45. If anyone thinks this is gambling watch the movie Rounders. I know my shit. I always expect to win. Playing against leagues with 10 to 14 teams. The stats say I CRUSH FANTASY FOOTBALL!

You're a champion at fantasy sports. *It means nothing!* It started as a fantasy of you playing football and it ended with you being a nerd winning a fantasy game.

You didn't run on a field. You never went to practice. You didn't study game film. You didn't pick up a real ball. You did nothing athletic at all. You don't own a real team. You don't have a real trophy. That you are a champion is make-believe. Who cares? Why would anyone brag about being good at fantasy football? It's embarrassing. You took the Baltimore Ravens defense this week? Wow, that's really smart seeing that the Ravens defense has been great since the year 2000. Take the NY Jets offense one week. That's a smart move since that side of the ball only plays one good game a year. Try to pick the one week they do that. You know what? How about this?

Go fuck yourself champ! And if I see you in a sports bar on a Sunday looking at your fantasy football stats on your iPad I'll smash it into pieces. The only thing you crush is cock!

Grown Man Mistakes

Here is a guy bragging about his promotion. He's another asshole who loves using the awful phrase—*crushing it.*

> I'm extremely excited I accepted a promotion with my company. Starting Friday I'll be the supervisor leading a sales team. #CrushingIt #GrownManMoves

Hashtag—Yech! Really?
Grown man moves?
I'm sure none of your friends have ever received a promotion. Yep, no one will doubt you any longer. Especially since you put a hashtag in front of *grown man moves*. Hashtags are for chicks, by the way. You're not crushing anything either. There was a guy before

you doing that job really shitty and getting paid too much money so they fired him and hired you for half the money he was making. It was a corporate move, asshole. This has nothing to do with it being a grown man move except for the head of the company who is a grown man made the move. The only thing you will be crushing in six months is your head into the wall when they get rid of you and hire the next asshole. Hashtag—fuck you!

Take Action!

Many of the self-appointed gurus on Facebook write updates about their plans to achieve certain goals. One piece of advice comes up frequently: *take action*!

Get Ready for Nothing!

Watch out, people. Here's a strong woman ready to *take action*:

> 🐼   Get ready! I'm going to do what makes me happy, and it's only getting more clear now!

Immediately after her post her friend comments:
Best mentality to have!
Then a guy posts a picture of Beyoncé with the title:
I'm not bossy, I'm the boss!
The Beyoncé meme is kind of ironic. Is she really a boss when she lets her husband cheat on her and then does nothing about it? That doesn't sound like a boss to me. That sounds like someone who is afraid to be alone and lets people walk all over her. Sounds like her overrated husband is the boss, but, getting back to this awful post, yep, this woman has inspired all of us!

Get ready? Get ready for what? I'm ready but nothing has happened since she posted this. You know what she's going to do to make her happy? Something dumb like taking a cooking class. She read about some cunt on *Huffington Post* that starting taking a cooking class and it made her so much happier now. It sounds like by her post that she is finally ending a relationship. That's a good time to learn how to cook when you have no one to cook for anymore, you dumb twat.

Bad Life Boss

This woman posted a picture of a cup of hot tea on top of a notebook. Her laptop is open for work. Then, she posted this caption:

> Parties. Events. Dinners. Dancing. All of these things sound so promising on a Saturday night. However, this is where I shall be spending my night. Must do what others don't so that I may have what others won't! Work hard now, play hard later! #BossBabe #Focus

Sounds to me like this woman had nothing to do on this Saturday night so she decided to stay in and get some work done instead. If she got invited to any of those events she would have gone in a second. Instead she tries to put up a brave front and tell her friends what a hard worker she is and make them feel guilty because they're out having fun on a Saturday night like most people do. You know she barely got any work done. After ten minutes she got bored, went on Amazon and bought a bunch of shit to fill the void in her empty life.

Chicks don't stay home on a Saturday night by themselves. That's the worst thing a woman can go through. They would rather go through menopause.

Work hard now, play hard later.

Why can't you work a little and then play a little? What the fuck is the difference? You're staying in on a Saturday night with a cup of tea. I'm sure you're super fun when you play hard. How do you play hard, by getting up at the crack of dawn to hit the local garage sales?

Set Goals!

We live in the age of productivity. Everyone has read a book or seen a video about getting organized. Setting goals is not life-changing advice. It's old, rehashed bullshit. Here are some awful examples from some awful human beings.

Improving My Nonsense

This was posted a few days before the New Year:

> 🏆 2016 will be a very selfish year. My time will be invested on improving myself. I want to become a better person physically and mentally.

Wow! What a fucking original New Year's resolution!

You, sir, are special! Just when I thought nobody wants to improve themselves you come along with this inspiring Facebook update.

It has been quite a while since you posted this. Did you become a better person? What did you do different? Are you in better shape? How's that head? Better mentally? *No? Nothing?* Do you still drink too much? Do you fuck random girls without a condom? Do you still steal at work? You do, huh? Hmmm. Sounds to me like you're the same piece of shit you were in 2015.

Wonder Woman & Her Untamed Ego

Get ready for this delusional asshole. Here's a woman letting us all know that she has conquered the problems of life. But before we get into what she wrote, let me give you a little back-story.

She refers to herself as *Wonder Woman* and her husband as *Superman*. She refers to her kids as *the natives*.

She doesn't have a job outside the home so she spends her day on Facebook bragging how *the natives* are so fucking smart and great. Meanwhile, Superman is busting his ass at work. She's at home raising the kids and cleaning up the place. It's a nonstop brag-fest with her and her updates like this:

> Taming the House Hydra today! On a side note, I come downstairs after getting ready for the day and I see the oldest native doing homework. I'm about to deliver justice and punishment when he proceeds to tell me that it's homework that is due NEXT Thursday. He said that he didn't want to have to worry about it during the break. Glad to know that my parenting skills are doing all right! Until later!

Good for your son but what the fuck did that have to do with you being a good parent? He did his homework a week in advance because he didn't want to wait until the last second. He was probably lying anyway. He was really on Snapchat and had his homework out to distract you. He was telling his friends how he can't wait until he turns eighteen because he has a mother that thinks she's Wonder Woman.

Here's the next update she posted:

> Wonder Woman is back with a magical new boot I have tamed the House Hydra. I have defeated the Lotus Eaters of Laundry and delivered justice to the Clutter Cyclops that has taken over since my downfall. Next on the list . . . BAKE! And lots of it! Until later!

You're telling me that you cleaned, did laundry, and now you're going to bake after all of that? *Get the fuck out of here!* Let me guess, your next post is going to be about what an amazing baker you are and how you cleaned up the mess all by yourself! This woman's face should be put on our currency when they update it. *Pure narcissism at its finest!*

Actually, this wonderful woman isn't saving the world, she's torturing it. She can't stop posting shit like this:

> I will be fabulous today! Despite the many things this Wonder Woman has to do I will do it looking fabulous, feeling fabulous, and sending vibes of fabulousity to all those I see. Why you may ask? Because I am who the world needs me to be! I am Wonder Woman!

No, we don't need you to be anything!

Superman needs you to be a good wife and good mom and take care of the kids. The rest of the world doesn't give a fuck about you! There're maybe forty people in the world that care about you. The rest of us don't know you, don't want to know you, and after reading these posts—hope you drop dead soon!

But you can't help yourself, can you? Here's another one:

> So remember that post I made a while back. Saying this Wonder Woman was going to work out for 100 days straight and wasn't going to miss a single day? Well, today marks 200 DAYS of not missing one single day. Wow! I actually have mini-triceps, biceps, and I can see my abs. My Georgia Peach is looking pretty fantastic, I must say. Here's to another 100 days of being absolutely curvaceous and fabulous and loving myself in every way. Until later!

Hmm! You think Wonder Woman is bragging here?

How does she do this? She cleans, bakes, takes care of the kids, and she doesn't miss a workout?

I will call *bullshit* on this one.

Nobody works out two hundred days in a row. All of this is bullshit. She likes reading fiction, and she writes it, too. Here's an example of one of her best bullshit stories:

> Talk about a confidence boost from the beach! A woman comes over and compliments my bathing suit. She said the color looks beautiful against my skin and it defines my curves. She said it was the best-looking bathing suit on the beach and all her friends agreed. They also couldn't believe the shape I had and asked me how many times a week I work out. They complimented me on how amazing I looked for a mom that has a few kids. Looking good and feeling good! Until later!

That never fucking happened!

A woman didn't come up to you to compliment your amazing *bathing suit* and how it *compliments your curves*. She didn't say it was the *best-looking bathing suit on the beach.*

Nobody said that. You are full of shit!

Women are jealous of other women. If they know your bathing suit looks good, they will tear it down. They don't know you. They will not walk up to you, out of the blue, and compliment you on having the best bathing suit on the beach.

Six chicks didn't walk up in a group and give you all of those compliments. It never happened!

You're a wonder at one thing—being a disaster of a human being. Think about that.

Until later!

CHAPTER FOUR

STRIP CLUB PARADISE

I grew up in Central New Jersey. Technically, our family was middle class but my lifestyle was more white trash. The middle-class part of my life was the nice suburban home, hardworking father, stay-at-home mother, and a conservative Catholic upbringing.

The white-trash part of me lived on the edge of the highway that cut through our traditional family neighborhood. This was where Jon Bon Jovi famously grew up. Route 35 in Sayreville.

Right around the corner from the nice houses and the local 7-11 was a horny teenager's dream. There were at least eight strip clubs in a three-mile radius. *The Marleybone Pub. The Go-Go Rama. Fantasies.* Every two blocks was another bar filled with dancers. This area was our white-trash mecca. A paradise lit up by strip club neon.

Because of my strict Catholic upbringing, I was sexually repressed. Stifling all of those sexual feelings messes with your head. I didn't get laid until one month before my eighteenth birthday. I didn't masturbate until I was twenty-one. Suffice it to say, I had my share of sexual hang-ups but I was in good company. All of my buddies were like me, crazy animals who desperately needed to blow a load.

I think it's true when people say Catholic kids are crazy. Sexually repressed kids build up a lot of anger and rage. If you clean your pipes the pent-up energy calms down but until then you stay nuts. That's my theory at least and it seemed to be true in my case. Of course, adults don't teach young boys how to remedy that situation so you have to figure it out yourself.

We found our answer at the strip clubs. I had a bad mustache and a mullet haircut. I couldn't talk to women unless they wanted to discuss baseball, football, or why Ozzy left Black Sabbath. So I had to pay to talk to girls.

Barmaid Babysitters

The first time I remember visiting a strip club was when I was fourteen. One of our friends bragged that a certain club near our home had served him beer. So, one afternoon I walked over there with two of my buddies to find out if the rumor was true.

Now, this place was an all-nude club. I'm still unclear on the laws and how they pull that off but I'm grateful we got in. When we walked in the first thing we saw was a dancer shoving a Heineken beer bottle in her snatch. *It was AMAZING!* It was the first time I ever wanted to drink a beer!

Sure, we had seen pictures in *Playboy* and *Penthouse,* but this was on a whole other level. We stepped up to the bar and ordered some beers.

"We'll take what *she's* having!"

The barmaid just laughed. She knew we were underage.

"Look, if you want to go over to that booth, I'll bring you some *sodas.*"

Well, shit. It wasn't beer, but they weren't kicking us out. We took her up on the offer and found some seats close to the performer.

All I can say is that it was a fantastic, insane moment in my life. I was a fourteen-year-old kid drinking a Coke in an all-nude bar with two of my best friends. It couldn't get better than that. These days, the barmaid would be arrested, prosecuted, exposed on CNN, and denounced by every parent with a social media account.

Here, no one bothered us. I sat there and experienced what it felt like to be jealous of a lubed-up longneck. To this day the only beer I drink is Heineken. Advertising really does work!

Double-Stuffing Dollars

Back in my day, the most common activity in the club was *stuffing*. A stripper comes over to flirt with you and you'd "stuff" her bra or panties by placing a rolled up dollar in her cleavage or in the elastic of her waistband.

One night, my brother thought up a way to get more out of our money.

"Let's pool our singles, cut them in half, roll them up tight, and use them to stuff!"

He was literally cutting into the stripper's profits. It was stupid and unnecessary, but we went along with the idea.

As long as you took the rolled up half-dollar bill and stuffed it quickly the dancer just assumed it was a regular dollar bill. There was only one problem.

"We have to make this quick!" someone said, "As soon as one of them finds out what we've done, she'll come storming out of that back room and bust us."

He was right. It wouldn't take long to figure out the young broke scumbags in the corner were the ones scamming the strippers. Our strategy became stuff and run!

We stuffed our half dollars, watched the tits bounce for a few minutes, guzzled our beer, and disappeared as fast as possible. It was a game to see how many times we could do it and not get caught. So, after hitting one club with our scam we drove down the street to another strip club and did it all again until we ran out of money.

I do regret not seeing the faces of those women when they unrolled those dollars. I'm sure they were thinking, *who in the fuck would do this?*

Well, we did it and got away with it! Guess they'll bring Scotch Tape to work from now on.

Lunch Break Lap Dances

During my strip club days, I worked as the delivery truck guy for Jacob's Hardware. I was the kid who drove their big panel truck and dropped off mulch, grass seed, and lawn mowers to the customers. It was a good job for me at the time because it allowed me freedom during the day. I found hundreds of tiny ways to waste my time while out on delivery.

When I was bored, I'd find a way to get my friend Chuck involved. He was a slob like me and I really liked hanging out with him. I'd tell the boss I hurt my back and I needed Chuck's help delivering the heavy shit. The boss always agreed. We'd take our time driving to the customer's house, usually stop for lunch at Burger King, and finally drop off the item.

The best days were when we got tips. If the customer were generous with us, we would drive straight to Club 516. This was a strip club on Route 516 less than a mile away from our work. It was risky stopping here. The hardware store was right down the road and you could see any car that was in the club parking lot. Thankfully, there was one spot in the back I could hide the truck. I laughed when I imagined people driving by wondering, *Why is the Jacob's Hardware delivery truck at the strip club?*

After a few weeks, we had mastered the strip club lunch break. We would get our tip. Buzz over to the club and buy one beer. We had to split it because we needed singles for the dancers. Usually, we'd get two stuffs and then finish our drink and head back to work with beer on our breaths. It was a fucking beautiful! Club 516 became one of my favorite strip clubs because of those memories. I wanted to have my son's christening there but, for some reason, I got backlash from my family.

Never Sit Near the Beer Cooler

There's a lot to learn if you want to enjoy your visit to a strip club. For instance, if I walk into a strip club and I see a guy sitting near the cash register I immediately know this guy is a rookie. Never sit there or where servers pick up drink orders. You are doing it all wrong if you sit around the bar clutter or next to the beer cooler.

You can't be part of the action here. The dancer is literally eight feet away from you. The barmaid working in this area may talk to you but she's going to be busy and cranky. This is no man's land! Move. Find an empty spot near the dancer's stage so her tits are an inch away from your face. That's how the professionals do it.

Always Go with the Minority

Here's another important strip club rule. If you want to get a good lap dance be careful who you pay to do it. In my expert opinion, you want a woman who puts effort into a lap dance. The rule of thumb is always go with the minority!

Never go with the white girl. She feels entitled and doesn't want to be there. She thinks she is too good for this line of work even though she's no better than anyone else. I've had long conversations with these women and I know them well. The conversation is always the same.

"I'm just working here because I'm saving to go back to school."
She's not!
"My grandmother is sick, that's why I work as a dancer!"

Nope, your grandmother is perfectly fine.

"I'm saving to buy a house!"

Lie!

"I'm going to open a nail salon."

Well, maybe the Asian Stripper is.

You spend all your money at the nail salon but you're not buying one.

You may have a good night and make some fast money but you take it to the mall the next day and buy shit you don't need. You feel good for three minutes. Then, you're right back to the self-loathing and broken dreams.

Let me repeat. *Go with the minority!*

The entitled white girls are train wrecks. Especially, the ones from overseas. In the tail end of my strip club days, the Russians invaded and it ruined the clubs. They were looking for rich guys and acted indifferent to everyone else. It sucked the fun out of the experience.

The black, Latina, or Asian woman has a different attitude. They take the business seriously. They save their money and work hard for every dollar. They have three kids at home, the power is out, they have a stack of bills, and they aren't sitting around conjuring up stupid dreams of opening a hair salon.

They approach their customers with a decent attitude. *Hey, you're my man and I'll take care of you if you pay me right!*

During that lap dance, you really believe you are the only man in the world they care about. Even if it's a fantasy, they sell it. Meanwhile, the white girl pretends she is grinding on you six inches above your crotch and while she stares at her freshly painted nails.

Reward the real working girls and you'll have the time of your life. Just don't go too far and try and pull a black girl's hair during the dance. You'll pull off her weave, she'll get all ghetto on you, and you'll lose your erection in the process.

ANNOYING HOTEL MAIDS

As a comedian, I'm on the road all the time. I have a strange schedule so when I check into a hotel room I always have the same conversation with the front desk.

"Look, just so you know, I'm only in town for two days. I work nights. I sleep in. I don't want to be bothered at any time during the day. So, I don't need maid service."

They always say the same thing.

"Just put the *Do Not Disturb* sign on the door and you won't have a problem, sir."

Can you guess what happens?

Nine o'clock in the morning, the phone rings.

"Do you need any service in your room, sir?"

"Don't I have the *Do Not Disturb* sign on the door?"

"Ah, yeah but we weren't sure if you need any maid service?"

"Oh, really? What does your *Do Not Disturb* sign say? 'Do Not Disturb' with a question mark?"

"Well, if you need any towels let us know!"

"I have seventeen towels in my room, unless a dam bursts in my room I won't need an eighteenth towel. When I'm home, I use the same towel for three weeks straight. I'm okay with the towels!"

"Okay sir, but if you need towels just call the front desk."

"Oh thanks, I wasn't sure where to get towels when I stay in a hotel. I thought I might have to do a Google search, find the local Bed Bath & Beyond, and go buy some!"

Hotel maids. Fucking brilliant. What would I do without them?

The Nipple Brush-Off

Pick your favorites. That's another unwritten rule in the strip club. There are so many girls floating around the club it's easy to get confused. Maybe one or two turn you on. A few have an attitude you don't like. At least one woman will spark your interest and that will be your favorite for the night. Spend time figuring out who that is and give her your money. Be warned. A few girls are determined to bug you.

Just an aside here, that's the great thing about a strip club, inflation never fucks up the prices at a strip club. Milk and bread cost more every year but strippers never raise their prices. You'll never hear a stripper say, "Can you give me $1.35 this time because Obamacare fucked me over!"

Anyway, it's sad when the annoying stripper is standing there begging and you are waiting for the hotter girl. You only have so many dollars and you want to save them for the girls you find attractive.

My friends and I had a solution for this that seemed to work. If a mediocre one stops by for some money I would blurt out, "I like your nipples. They look like my grandmothers!"

She'd give me a strange look, "I don't want to know how you know how your grandmother's nipples look."

To make sure she didn't come back, I'd add, "Because we shower together!"

If that didn't make her go away, we'd start a bullshit conversation. The trick here is to babble nonsense as loud and intense as possible. All the while, you ignore the stripper that's bellied up to your table.

"Can you believe the Jets lost?"

"No man, I can't believe it!"

"Yeah that fucking sucks. What about that Giants game?"

"I didn't see that, but this weather is insane, how's it still raining?"

"Yeah, I watched the news and they didn't say shit about a storm!"

Now, at some point you will hear the stripper's voice saying, "Hi guys!"

Don't stop! Block her!

"Holy shit, I thought we were going to have a flood."

If you hear another, "Hi guys!" Continue ignoring her until she gives up.

"I couldn't believe that play in the third quarter! Holy shit, what a pass!"

Eventually the dancer will walk away.

Maybe I hurt her ego by ignoring her but I'm waiting for the hot stripper with no dents in her ass as my friend Dave says. Dave appreciates an ass without cellulite.

All of this may seem harsh but feelings get hurt in the strip club. Strippers' feelings get hurt. Your feelings will get hurt. It's just part of the game. Accept the dark side of the fantasy, shut the fuck up, and stuff another dollar. Or, rip a single in half and stuff two!

Driving Dancers

Eventually, I went from strip club regular to strip club employee. When the Playpen decided they would be a strip club during the day and rock club at night, I became their main DJ. The job was noon to six, three days a week, and the pay sucked. This was before DJs made eight hundred a night. The most I ever made was seventy-five bucks for a shift.

However, the pay wasn't the problem I had with this job. The problem was that I developed a serious infatuation with one dancer. That misguided crush led me into an even worse job—strip club driver!

The driver is the guy who schleps the stripper to and from work because she has fifteen points on her driving record, or she has no car, or her piece-of-shit vehicle is always in the shop. Usually, she's recovering from a DWI or gets too hammered after work and needs someone to take her home. Suffice it to say, the driver is the biggest loser in the whole strip club system.

I was naive and thought being the driver would impress the dancer I liked. I thought she would think of me as a nice guy, get turned on by all the attention I was showing her, and then let me get in her pants. That was nothing but a pathetic fantasy.

When a stripper gets off the stage and gets dressed to go home, they dress like a slob. If you've ever seen a stripper come out of the club after her shift then you know it's a big disappointment. She wears a huge T-shirt down to her knees, her long beautiful hair is in a fucking bun, makeup is off, and all you see are the zits and the bruises she gets from pole dancing. Her hot ass is gone because she's wearing sweats that are twenty times too big. The hot stripper you saw on stage suddenly morphs into a cranky homeless chick.

When she comes out, she gets in the car with three suitcases full of shit, reeks of cigarettes, and of course wants to go to the fucking diner because she's starving. She was a nine up on stage but now under the fluorescent lights stuffing her pimpled face with bacon, she's maybe a four. She sits there spewing her delusions.

"That new girl stole my shoes and my G-string. I'm going to go tell the manager. I can't believe this shit."

I'm sitting there listening to this horseshit, meanwhile I had to get up at seven thirty for work and I'm out at three thirty hoping I'll get laid.

She has five hundred bucks in singles but I'm afraid to ask her for gas money because I don't want to jinx the insanely remote chance she will give me a blowjob. It was that moment I knew I had hit rock bottom. There was nothing worse than being the strip club driver. When a cranky chick is wearing no makeup, has her hair in a bun, and is eating shitty food the last thing on her mind is later on getting on all fours for you.

Awful Facebook Rule #4:
Post a "Feel-Sorry-for-Me" Update

I hope you laughed at my pathetic strip club stories and didn't feel bad for me.

Yet, today when you look on Facebook half of the posts are pathetic pleas for undeserved sympathy. I call these shitty posts *feel-sorry-for-me* updates. If you've heard any of my podcasts, you know I rant about these all the time. One warning, reading some of these examples will make you want to punch the nearest person next to you.

Weight-Loss Amputations

Here's a pathetic example of the feel-sorry-for-me update. Read this and see if you think she's fishing for sympathy.

> 🏆 I found the solution to being so horribly overweight. I'm cutting off my legs, yep, that should do it!

I would pay someone to respond with a comment that says, "Great idea. Let me know if you need to borrow my chainsaw!" All her friends ignore this shit because it's just pathetic. In fact, she had this post up for five days and no one liked it or commented on it because this feel-sorry-for-me shit aggravates people.

I know she's expecting her friends to write things like: *Oh, you look great. You don't need to lose weight. You're beautiful.* But, here's my advice. Just write what you mean:

Can someone please tell me I'm not fat, so I can feel better about myself.

Don't dummy this shit up so that people are worried about you. I'm sure a few people wondered, *Is she really going to do this? She needs help!*

You could stop eating!

Just a suggestion.

Go on the Internet and do a little research on how to eat healthy. It's not like you have to go to the library to get this information.

You know what, that's not a bad idea. Log out of Facebook, get off your ass, and walk to library for some exercise. Just do it before you amputate those beefy legs. Hopefully, she won't pass an Arby's on the way to the library. I have a feeling a #7 Special is in her future!

This Mom Makes Me Puke

This is a typical feel-sorry-for-me mom. They're constantly complaining about all the time they spend being a parent.

> I don't care if I suck at parenting on every level. Cleaning up a giant pile of teenage vomit off the kitchen floor wins me a fucking trophy. The end. You're welcome for this post.

First of all, you say, *You're welcome for this post.* Who exactly is going to thank you for this post? Most people will want to vomit themselves after reading your post. So, you're reminding everyone, here at the beginning, that you suck as a parent. Why don't you try to be a better one, then? If you think cleaning up your kid's vomit earns you a trophy, you really suck as a parent. Most moms know this is part of being a parent.

Did you bitch when you had to wipe your kid's ass? Imagine how many trophies you deserve for all of that work. It sounds like you really never intended to be a parent. You should have thought about the repercussions before you opened your legs that fateful night.

You're welcome!

GARY FROM FLORIDA: THE ITALIAN STALLION

Gary from Florida is good with money! He's owned several businesses and always makes great investments. If you listen to my podcasts, you've heard about his wild times owning a liquor store and you know he's a very successful guy.

Now, I was taught a man pays for dinner when you are on a date. It was drilled into me you shouldn't be a cheapskate. Give your date the best of everything and you increase your chances of having sex!

Gary has an opposite approach. He keeps the cost of getting laid down to the bare minimum. And, he's quick to make sure the woman contributes.

One hand washes the other, fella. If you're good in bed, the woman should pay her fair share of everything else!

Gary from Florida is pragmatic. According to him, you shouldn't waste time and money on dinner when you'd rather be in bed eating pussy. In fact, Gary has a reliable secret for handling dinner dates that any man can use.

Look here fella, if you want to make a woman cream her panties, invite her over to your house and cook her a real Italian meal. At Walgreens, you can get a bottle of Barolo wine for about $3.98. Pick up two just in case you want to do this twice in one week.

Next, grab a couple cans of SpaghettiOs. Right before your date arrives, open the cans, and heat them up in a fancy skillet. Let them simmer until they're ready to eat.

Now, I grow my own vegetables and herbs. If you don't, start a small garden. It saves money! If you don't have time for that grab some fresh basil at the store. Chop it up and set it aside. Plate the pasta. Dust the SpaghettiOs with Parmesan cheese. Sprinkle on the chopped basil and set the table.

You're almost there, fella. Now, open the Walgreens wine. If you do it right, the whole process should take about 10 minutes and cost you about $10 bucks. Nothing to it. Follow my rules and you'll have a dinner that will make any woman beg for the Bonecrusher!

Works every time!

Please Stop Breathing

The common cold is called the *common* cold because everyone on the planet has had it in their life. Here is an adult woman who wants us to feel sorry for her because she caught it. Why?

> I can't breathe. Ugh, stupid cold. Why don't you find someone else to drag down and be miserable? More medicine!

Yuck!

I'm sick. Feel bad for me, please. I'm a grown-up but feel bad for me.

Look lady, I apologize. We asked around and couldn't find anyone else who would take this virus for you. We tried hard but all the conversations went like this:

Hey you want to be miserable and take this cold from this chick?

No, sorry, I have work and kids and other shit I really have to do!

Yeah, I know but she's really miserable. Could you just take it for her?

No, I don't want it either, they said.

Dammit, why won't anyone take this cold for this woman, she's suffering!

I will take her cold from her as long as she blows me. I know she can't breathe but that shouldn't affect her swallowing!

Praying for Continued Pain

For this one a woman posted a picture of a big scar she has on her wrist. The picture is super nasty. Nobody needs to see this shit but she thinks it's newsworthy.

 Cast is off! I'm free! Check out the scar! Surgeons like permanent marker!

Of course, here come the sympathy comments. You ready for them?

Ouch!

Oh no, painful!

You poor girl, what did you do?

Hope it feels better than it looks!

Now, was any of that shit necessary? It's just mindless drivel. Someone else commented:

I will pray for continued healing!

You're not going to pray for continued healing.

Can you imagine a priest approaching this woman who dragged her nine-year-old son with her to church while she is praying?

I see you've been sitting here a long time, is everything all right?

Well, my friend posted a picture of her scar on Facebook and I told her I would pray for continued healing. So, I got in my car and ran down here.

Is it not healing right? Does she need more surgery?

No, she just posted a picture, and I said I would pray for continued healing.

Maybe you should pray for something a little more important like world peace.

Well, she didn't write about that in her Facebook post.

I'm sorry, you need to leave now because you're wasting God's time with your dumb requests! But, feel free to leave your son for me.

Unimportant Feelings

I can sum up this Facebook post as an unimportant post about being unimportant.

 Feeling unimportant! ☹

There is no etiquette for these fucking feel-sorry-for-me posts. Are you supposed to *like* the fact that someone feels unimportant? Should you give her a thumbs up? If you did, does that mean you agree with her? Isn't that going to make her feel worse?

Let me guess, you're feeling unimportant because a bunch of people are out together and they are taking pictures, posting them online, and you feel left out. Maybe it is because whenever you go out with them you cause problems and they don't feel like dealing with it this time. You only feel important when you cause drama. You should feel important now, you made my book with your awful post!

CHAPTER FIVE

PRANKING LIKE IT'S 1999

Fast forward to 1999, I'm living with my girlfriend and my good friend, Jim Norton, in a dingy apartment. Jim and I were both comedians, so we rented something on the edge of New Jersey to be close to New York City and its comedy club scene.

At this point, I'd been doing standup for about seven years. Jim had put in about the same time. All of our gigs were shitty. We barely made a living. Our rent was eight hundred a month, and we had to split it three ways to keep a roof over our heads.

I would sleep in every morning because I had nothing going on in my career. But I would always answer the phone in case it was a new opportunity. *Nope!* It was always a fucking *telemarketer*.

I hated these scumbags, so I would try to keep them on the phone as long as possible.

One day, my buddy Don Jamieson asked me to put him on three-way so he could listen in.

"You're on to something," he said, "You need to be recording these calls!"

After Don encouraged me, I let a few friends listen to the recordings. The reaction was always positive. People hated telemarketers, so they loved hearing me turn the tables on them.

The Fortunate Birth of Special Ed

The next day, I walk over to the Radio Shack and buy a phone call recorder for about eighty bucks. This was way before the digital age and the device used a regular-sized cassette to store the calls but it did the job I needed it to do. I hooked it up and waited for the next telemarketer to call.

I had an advantage because as long as you don't curse, or tell a telemarketer you don't want the product, they can't hang up. Ending the call prematurely is frowned upon because hanging up means you are passing up a potential sale. Most of the time, their calls end with, "Fuck you, and never call here again!" So, when they got me on the phone they were just happy to be talking to someone that sounded sane.

One day my calls were going nowhere. I was having these super long conversations but the telemarketer's reactions were boring. It seemed they were beating me at my game. At one point, I was so frustrated I acted like a retard. *Would they stay on the phone*, I wondered.

The telemarketer said, "Would you like to order our product?"

I yelled, "Yaaaaaaaayyyyyyyyy!"

The telemarketer asked again and I would just repeat myself. "Yaaaayyyy!"

I couldn't believe they stayed on the line. It proved they didn't give a shit who they sold their products to, they had to make the sale.

One day, a guy called me to sell me a Bose radio for $350.

I told him, "Yaaaayyyy! Hold on let me go get my piggybank and see if I have enough money."

The guy stayed on the phone as I counted pennies. That was the moment I knew that this make-believe Ed would be *special*.

Terrorizing Telemarketers

Before I put my first *Terrorizing Telemarketers* CD out, I decided to test market it with my family. I remember playing the calls for my seventy-six-year-old grandmother, my mom, and my ten-year-old nephew. When I had all three of them laughing, I knew I was onto something.

I started by printing a thousand CDs and sold them after my shows. At the least, I thought the album would get my name out there. Also, I knew I could make a few bucks to pay for gas and lap dances.

Eventually, I signed a shitty deal with a small record label and got my CD in the stores.

GROWN MEN & BASEBALL MITTS

A while back, I went to an Orioles game at Camden Yards in Baltimore. While I was there, I sat next to two guys in their mid-thirties holding baseball mitts. If you are with your son and your son says, "Dad, bring your mitt to the game maybe we can catch a foul ball!" no problem, that makes sense. But, when you are going with your friend and you are both grown men there is no reason to bring your fucking mitts to the game.

These guys were also scoring the game with a scorebook. *NOBODY GIVES A SHIT!* What are you going to do with that? Are you framing the scorecard? Are you going to show your friends when you get home?

"Hey, I scored the game last night you want to look at it?"

"NO!"

Why are you bringing your mitts to the game? There is no reason for that. Just go into the souvenir shop and buy a ball and go post it on Facebook with a caption, *I caught a ball at the game!*

Also, these guys were drunk and hitting on every chick that walked past them. I was thinking, what's going to happen if they do meet women that are interested? Can you imagine that?

"Hey, the game's over let's go to one of the bars outside of Camden Yards!"

They get to the door and bouncer says, "You can't bring your baseball mitts into this bar!"

"Yeah, but we went to the game! Come on, man!"

"It says here on your IDs that you are both thirty-five years old. This must be fake because there is no way thirty-five-year-old grown men would bring baseball mitts to a game to catch a foul ball. And, why in the hell do you have a scorebook?"

Then the girls go in and the guys are left outside.

Or they say, "Hey girls, can you wait we are going to put our mitts and our scorebook in the car and we will be right back!"

Fucking pathetic! These guys are never getting laid. Stop it with the mitts. Just go buy a damn ball.

Awful Facebook Rule #5: Kiss Your Spouse's Ass Online

My mother and father are two people who have a legitimate reason to gloat about their relationship on social media.

They were a traditional couple. My father worked. My mother stayed home and raised seven kids by herself. All the kids were close in age. So, you can imagine how fucking hard that was with seven small kids driving her crazy. She had to cook, clean, and do laundry for everyone.

My mom was also athletic so when we got home from school she was in the backyard with us playing sports. After that, she had to cook dinner for the whole family.

My father worked his ass off to provide for a family of nine people. He had to make sacrifices by working long hours and missing time with his family. You never heard him bitching and moaning about any of it.

In fact, neither one of them demanded praise for doing what was expected of parents. Contrast that with the multitude of assholes on Facebook complaining about having to do the simplest of chores. Parents with one child think they should get a fucking award for heating up a microwave dinner or doing one load of laundry.

Even if there had been Facebook back in my parents' day, I can guarantee my parents would have never posted shit like, *Hey, I just cooked ravioli for my seven children!* No one cares.

I have a theory that if you have a good relationship you should stay away from Facebook altogether. You're just asking for trouble and unnecessary drama. Any couple that is happy in their relationship is not going to run to Facebook and tell everyone. They're too busy enjoying themselves in that moment.

Unfortunately, there is a whole subsection of Facebook users that love broadcasting personal interactions and conversations on social media. Because of all of this, my fifth rule for making Facebook awful is *Kiss Your Spouse's Ass Online.*

Angelic Assholes

Here's another way people use Facebook to brag. When they post this shit, they are saying, *I have the perfect partner and my relationship is better than yours!*

Take the next guy as an example. This ass sends his woman a picture of a couple with a sunset in the background. The couple in the picture is holding hands and looking into each other's eyes. This guy tags his chick and posts a caption that says:

When the angels ask what I love most about life, I'll say
YOU!

Of course, these fuckers are Facebook friends because that is a requirement if you want to kiss your spouse's ass online. The woman gets notified and writes back:

OMG! You couldn't be more perfect for me!

First, this woman is at least fifty and she's writing *OMG!* like she's a teenager. The premise of her man's note is even worse. He's suggesting angels will interrogate us when we die and we better say something nice about our significant other.

How does he know the angels are going to ask us that? Is he saying the angels greet us at heaven's gate like bouncers at a club? Will they demand our identification? Will they quiz us because they're suspicious we're trying to get into heaven with a fake ID?

"What's your birthday? What's your middle name? What's your street address? *What did you love most about life?*"

Is that what the angels do? I was raised Catholic and I've never heard anyone talk about this. I've been with religious people like my aunts and uncles when they were facing death. They had their priests with them in those moments and I've never heard any of them say *When you die the angels will ambush you with a quiz. Let's go over your answers because you need to get ready!*

Also, you look like you are in your early forties, which means you have more years on this planet. Let's say you break up in about six months and then two years later you find the woman of your dreams. You marry her and live with her for another thirty years before you die around seventy. In that scenario, I don't think you will tell the angels that the best part of your life was a girl you dated for six months.

If the angels ask me what I liked most about life, I'll tell them about the threesome I pulled in 1993. If they ask me what I hated most in life, I'll tell them about your dumb Facebook post!

Yuck! Other People Can Read This

Here is another asshole writing to his chick:

> I love you! I would do anything for you, anytime, for any reason!

Then his chick likes it, *of course*, and writes:

Awwwwwwww!

Here's the best part. One of their male friends writes:

You know other people can read this right? Yuuuucccckkkk!

That's fucking beautiful! Good for him! I would love to know their response to his comment. I imagine the first guy got mad, *Dude what the fuck? I was just trying to score points with my girlfriend. Why'd you write that?*

He wrote it because you are a fucking insecure ASSHOLE that's why! Why couldn't you text her that message? You wouldn't do anything for her at anytime for any reason. You might in that moment and that's it. Wait until you guys go out, get drunk, get in a big fight, and you wake up the next morning hung-over with her telling you she's made brunch reservations with her corny friends. I guarantee you'll tell her to fuck off!

JIMMY & JESUS

I've interviewed my mother a few times for my podcasts. It's interesting to hear her perspective on what I was like growing up. *You were so cute Jimmy when you were young. Everyone loved being with you because you were always running. You were doing it to make them*

laugh, once you had an audience forget about it, you would keep act-
ing silly. Your son is the same way. The apple doesn't fall far from the
tree. Whenever he has an audience, he keeps going. Very entertaining!
He likes to make everyone laugh. He's a born comedian, you grew into a
being a comedian!

It is even more fascinating hearing her thoughts on life and religion. She's a very devout woman and a serious Catholic but if you
ever listen to these podcasts, you'll understand she's not judgmental. Her number-one concern is making sure she does nothing
that would be offensive to Jesus.

For instance, one time someone gave me a Buddha statue as
a gag gift. I left it on my desk at home. About a day later, I came
home and it had a sock covering it. That was my mom. She was
making sure anything that may be disrespectful to Jesus was kept
out of the home or her life. There is only one problem with that.
Her son is an R-rated comedian.

Your father heard you on Howard Stern so that was good. I didn't lis-
ten to it. I don't listen to things like that because there is too much cursing.
I never watch or go to see anything that is R-rated. I only watch PG-13
or PG films. I like to think there is someone bigger than me watching over
us. If Jesus were a guest in my house, I wouldn't watch anything like that
so I don't do it when I'm alone. I don't think he would be mad at me. It
wouldn't stop me from getting into heaven. I just don't believe in doing it.

The way my mother thinks about her faith is very respectable.
She's not some holy roller who condemns people because they
don't believe or act like she does. She never made my father feel
guilty for watching his favorite R-rated movie *My Cousin Vinny.*
She's wouldn't think of condemning me for what I do. But her
strong faith has one funny consequence, she's only seen her professional comedian son perform his stand-up material twice and
both times they were the cleanest shows I've ever done. I did it
because I didn't want to make my mom uncomfortable while she
was in the crowd. Plus, I needed her to give me a ride home!

Ham-Style Holiday

This next jerk-off loves bragging about how hard he works. You would think he's the only guy in the whole world with a job.

> 🦀 So, I can't wait to plan a much-needed VACAY with my girlfriend. First, I need to rock it through the holidays HAM style. Then the ocean awaits!

His girlfriend comments underneath his post.

You work so hard. You definitely deserve a great vacation! Love you!

A response was so important she couldn't wait until they got home.

What's really going on is these couples are so insecure they comment on each other's posts to let all their friends know they are in a serious relationship. It's a subtle way of letting people know stay the fuck away from that person! That's my partner, not yours!

These posts don't really protect relationships, they make them unstable. Other people, usually women, see these types of posts, go home, and berate their partner. *Why don't you post comments about me on Facebook? They are so in love why aren't we like that?*

Back to this ass, why would a guy use the word *vacay*? Even women cringe at that word. He writes, "I need to rock it through the holidays HAM style." HAM is an acronym for hard as a motherfucker. It's like the horrific word *beast mode* and means get the fuck out of my way because I'm out of control.

How does anyone rock it through the holidays HAM style? Dude, you won't do the holidays any differently than the rest of us. Everybody does the same thing. You travel, visit family, and buy presents.

Do these things if you want to be hard as a motherfucker during the holidays:

- Cut the line at Macy's and yell, *Get the fuck out of the way. I'm rocking it HAM style for the holidays!*
- When you want a Christmas tree rip it out of the ground by the roots!
- Drive 90 mph on Christmas Day to get to where you're going. Cut off traffic. Force cars off the road! Speed by and give them the finger!

Will this guy do any of these things? *Nope!* He wants us to think he's a hard motherfucker but he's not! He'll wait in line until it's his turn just like every other schlub. He'll sit in traffic like everyone else, and the tree he buys will be already cut and out of the ground. I hope on your much-needed *vacay* somebody beats you up *ham-style!*

The Gift of Bullshit

Here's a woman bragging about her wonderful husband just to make all the other people that follow her on Facebook envious and jealous and sad about their own relationship.

> Woke up this morning and realized my husband had placed little notes all over the house for my birthday. It was fun finding them all. I love him!

She shares a picture of a pile of pink Post-it Notes. There are five different pictures showing notes all over the house. One is on the Xbox. One is on the coffeepot. They say things like: *You are beautiful! You are my everything!* I hope the last one read, *I'm leaving you for your friend.*

Let's break this down. He did this because he ran out of gift ideas. His wedding anniversary was in November. He had to buy her nine different things for Christmas. Six weeks later was Valentine's Day.

Mother's Day is in May. That means there is more shit he has to buy her. Let me see if I can get by with her birthday by writing corny shit on little pieces of paper. Good for you dude, but fuck your wife for posting that nonsense.

GARY FROM FLORIDA: DON'T EAT THE GIRL SCOUT COOKIES, EAT THE BOX

Gary from Florida is a middle-aged guy that usually has several women in rotation. He's not a cold-hearted man, he's open to having a long-term relationship, and he loves women. He just doesn't like to get involved with their children.

If a woman has a kid it ain't bad, it just ain't for me!

He believes a house should be a kid-free zone. A simple in-and-out strategy is the best policy when dating women. You don't want to set up a situation in which a woman assumes it is okay to bring her kid. In other words, this is no place to eat cookies; this is where you eat the box.

I don't really like kids because they interfere with my routine. But, I can accept them if I'm dating a woman long-term. As long as the kid don't fucking come over!

One girl I was dating had a kid in the Brownies or Girl Scouts and I had to buy fourteen boxes of Girl Scout Cookies. That's not for me, fella. Don't call me Daddy; do you know what I mean? Fucking brutal! I'm just the guy fucking your mom.

I've asked him about a typical scenario single guys eventually face. You're dating a woman for many months. It's been going great. She has a kid but that hasn't caused a problem for you. After some time, she asks you to go to the kid's volleyball game. What do you do?

Easy. "Sorry, I'm busy that night! I have to do something on the computer."

What if she asks you again two nights later?

> *"Sorry, I'm in a hockey league on Playstation 4. We have an important game!"*
>
> So, there's no way you would get involved with the kid?
>
> *If this woman drops on her hands and knees to blow me, I might consider it.*
>
> But, you most likely wouldn't do it?
>
> *If she says, you know what I will give you later tonight? My beautiful brown eye! There's only one response to that: I'm going to the game! Hell, I'll even pump the fucking volleyball up for them!*

The One Facebook Post I Love

This next post may prove that Facebook can be used in a good way. Someone sent it for my podcast about *Awful Facebook Posts* but I don't find it awful. In fact, considering all the posts I've ever read, this may be my favorite of all time. The woman writes:

> You would think after being together for two years, living together, having two kids, and being a stepdad, that your boyfriend would stop trying to fuck other girls! But no, he just can't stop messaging other women! Get a fucking grip . . .

She inserts the dude's real name here but I'll leave that out. She continues:

> People should know what kind of person you are! It is 9 in the goddamn morning! Here's my boyfriend, the father of my kids, messaging girls he wants to fuck!

So nobody likes this post because who in their right mind would "like" this embarrassment? I'm sure everyone is reading it because they can't believe their eyes, but no one is stupid enough to say anything. Surprisingly, the first person to respond is the guy she is calling out, the boyfriend she found cheating. He writes:

Yeah, put this out there for everyone to see!

He doesn't defend himself or apologize. So, she responds:

Exactly, why be ashamed? Own up to the scumbag you are!

Call him out! Why not? She has every right to do this. She has two kids with this motherfucker. Can you imagine her morning? She's probably getting the kids ready for school. It's pure chaos and this guy is messaging chicks while she does all the heavy lifting. She catches him flirting, goes ballistic, and calls him out. Good for her!

Everybody should do that. *Seriously!* It might make someone think twice. What's crazy is he doesn't call her or talk to her in person? Instead, this idiot writes back to her on Facebook so everyone assumes he's guilty. Don't have kids with someone if you still want to fuck other people. When you have a kid it isn't about you anymore, motherfucker.

They have studies warning you about the negative effects of social media on your relationships:

> One in five divorces involve the social networking site Facebook, according to a new survey by the American Academy of Matrimonial Lawyers. A staggering 80 percent of divorce lawyers have also reported a spike in the number of cases that use social media for evidence of cheating.*

There is too much temptation on Facebook. It's all just bragging and showing off. If you are even the slightest bit interested in cheating, watch out!

---

* David Gardner, "The Marriage Killer: One in Five American Divorces Now Involve Facebook," http://www.dailymail.co.uk/news/article-1334482/The-marriage-killer-One-American-divorces-involve-Facebook.html.

What's the bottom line? There are what I call snipers out there trying to break up your relationships because they are jealous of your happiness.

Another article suggests married couples on Facebook should have rules about how to handle their accounts.

> You need to password-protect your marriage. No joke. This means that your husband or wife should be able to log onto your Facebook account at a moment's notice, any time of the day or night, especially when you are not there. Aside from, perhaps, planning a surprise party for your husband, if you are keeping anything "secret" from him in terms of your online interactions with other men, you are heading down a slippery slope.
>
> How to avoid it? Simple: He should know your password and, of course, if he has a Facebook account, you should know his. This rule isn't intended to foster "snooping" or paranoia, but it will help you ensure transparency and honesty with your husband or wife when it comes to your dealings with others online.
>
> Guys, knowing that your wife can at any time read anything you write on your Facebook page or your inbox messages will have a very clarifying effect on what you write. In other words, abiding by this rule will help you avoid situations in which you might be tempted to say something you wouldn't want your wife to see.*

If you are single and want to meet people on Facebook, fine, go for it. If you are married, follow this plan. No secrets. No passwords on Facebook or phones. Live like you have nothing to hide. If you think this is too much work, close your account and live your life instead of posting nonsense about it. I would ask the girl I'm dating now for all of her passwords, but she's too young to have a phone!

---

* Patrick Madrid, "If You're Married and You're on Facebook, You Should Read This," http://patrickmadrid.com/if-youre-married-and-youre-on-facebook-read-this/.

CHAPTER SIX

FLORENTINE'S GOT TALENT!

After *Terrorizing Telemarketers* was released, I felt my career was on the right track. I was proud of the reaction it got from people but I was still a long way from the next level in my career.

Thankfully, my next break was huge. My good friend Don Jamieson introduced me to Gary Dell'Abate, the producer of *The Howard Stern Show*. After a bit of discussion, Don and I met Gary at his office and dropped off a copy of my *Terrorizing Telemarketers* album.

Gary had piles and piles of CDs stacked on his desk. "If it's funny, we'll play it on the air. That's the most I can promise you," he said.

I figured he was just being nice by saying he would listen to it. I was such a huge fan of Stern I didn't really care what came of the meeting. I was just happy to see his studio.

The next morning I wake up to find my voicemail filled with messages. Friend after friend had called to tell me that Howard Stern was playing tracks from *Terrorizing Telemarketers* and laughing his ass off. His whole staff was going crazy for the material.

On one message, I could hear Stern saying, "Who is this guy, Gary? These calls are incredible. We got to get this guy in the studio. I've never heard anything like this!"

Two weeks later, I get an invitation to be a guest on the show. The day is burned in my memory—July 18, 2001. That day changed my career forever.

I checked the sales figures for my CD the night before my scheduled appearance. My ranking had plummeted to 282,483. That translated to about five sales per week.

The next day after my appearance on the show it shot up to #2 on Amazon!

The Backstreet Boys were the only band ahead of me. I believe I would've been #1 but at some point my website crashed. Stern kept sending his listeners to *jimflorentine.com* to buy the CD and because I had limited bandwidth, it couldn't handle the demand and my site crashed within two hours.

When *Billboard* magazine's Internet Charts came out, they listed *Terrorizing Telemarketers Volume One* at #17. U2 was ahead of me at #16 and the Dave Matthews Band was behind me at #18. I just imagined there were people reading this and asking who the fuck is Jim Florentine? Is this a new band? I got great pleasure out of that.

Believe me, I was asking the same question. *How the fuck did this happen?*

After that appearance on the show, I went from playing shitty bars and old VFW halls to performing in the top comedy clubs around the country.

Awful Facebook Rule #6: Pretend Things Are People

Rule Six for *How to Be Awful on Facebook* is *Pretend Things Are People*. These are the posts in which people talk about the days of the week and other inanimate objects as if they were humans. It's hard to find something more fucking annoying or corny.

The same boring people that want to discuss the weather with you at the grocery store are the type of people leaving these shitty posts.

Dicking Days of the Week

Stalking Monday

This post is brutal.

> ℧ Dear Monday, why are you following Sunday? Don't be a stalker.

Dear Jerk-off, if we change Monday so it's not following Sunday then we have to put another day of the week in its place. That day would stalk Sunday too. Not sure what to do here because there has to be a day that follows Sunday.

This guy's post was up for eight hours and had no comments and no one liked it. I wonder why?

You know he thought this was so damn clever and kept checking his page to see who commented. Imagine him at a restaurant with his wife looking at his phone during dinner. His wife gets annoyed that he's not paying attention to her. She starts bitching at him. He's upset and confused. He thought everyone would think that dumb post was so funny.

Meanwhile, his wife begins to think he's cheating because he keeps looking at his phone. I hope his wife leaves him on a Sunday and then on Monday fucks his best friend.

Fucking Friday

> I plan on making Friday my bitch this week! Have a great Friday everyone!

How is Friday going to be your bitch, sir? Tell me exactly what you will do. Are you going to take control of it because that's how you make something your bitch?

Are you going to take Friday away from everybody else and make it yours and only your bitch? So nobody else in the world is allowed to enjoy Friday? That doesn't seem fair. Is Friday is going to blow you? Is Friday going to drive you around because you're drunk and you don't want to get a DWI? I doubt that Friday knows how to drive a car.

If Friday were your bitch you would make it run errands for you. Are you doing that? Didn't think so! You're not going to make Friday your bitch. It's going to be like every other Friday, whatever lame shit you do every Friday you'll do this day, too. Okay, bitch?

Ruining Random Objects

Burying Dignity

This is from a woman with too much time on her hands.

> ✝ Funeral services to be determined. She was reliable, trustworthy, and made me money. She lasted longer than anyone anticipated. I trusted her with private information and she never gave away my secrets. Please join me as we say goodbye to my laptop. Feeling Sick! ☹

Why do I have to join you in saying good-bye to your laptop? I don't know it, I never met it, or if I did, your laptop wasn't memorable in the least.

Your laptop shit the bed so you have to buy a new one. Wow, I feel bad for you. That's never happened to anyone else. And, how can you tell if it's a she or a he?

I hope mine is a she because it watches me jerk off a lot. She's a trooper because she takes it in the face sometimes. If it's a male laptop, I'd like to take this opportunity to apologize to it. Hey man, I'm sorry. I know I've given you a facial a few times. I really apologize! Please don't flame out on me before I back up my hard drive.

Tequila Talking

> Dear Tequila, we had a deal last night you were supposed to make me funnier smarter and a better dancer. I saw the video we need to talk!

That's funny, right? *That's a good one!*

Why would you get smarter if you drink tequila? Do people who have to take a big test the next day go down to the bar and have a few shots to get ready for the exam?

Do the contestants on *Dancing with the Stars* drink tequila before they dance? I've read most of your other posts. Nothing will make you funnier or smarter. You'll always be a fucking dud!

Stuffing Ugly Sweaters

Here's one from a guy who's wearing a goofy outfit in his picture.

> This year's ugly Christmas sweater has not found me yet. I know it must be out there looking for me somewhere. I've come across a few potentials but not the one. I still miss the one I broke up with a few years ago and no others have come close. Like all good love affairs, I'm patiently waiting for the right one to come along but I'm not settling for a mediocre ugly Christmas sweater!

Why not settle for a mediocre sweater? I looked at your pictures and you settled for a mediocre girlfriend. You're not good looking either so you don't really need an ugly sweater to get noticed. Just get a regular sweater and put it over your head to hide your mediocre face.

Fuck That Fridge

> I can't take this long distance relationship anymore. Fridge, you're coming to my room.

I'd say there is a 98 percent chance this person is a horrendous slob.

Only a fat and lazy person would think it's a long-distance relationship when the object is in the next room over.

His profile picture is an image of a sunset, which means that he's a fat fuck. It's like when a girl uses a picture of her cat for her profile picture—you know what the deal is.

This guy probably likes the sunset going down because that means dinnertime, followed by dessert, followed by a midnight snack, followed by his finger down his throat over the toilet.

GARY FROM FLORIDA: JAMMING THE DUMPER

There is zero doubt about Gary from Florida's favorite sexual activity. Anal sex is his best-loved pastime. If he was a poet, he would write an ode to the ass because anal sex is more than an addiction to Gary, it's a personal calling. In his podcast interviews, he often says, *I'm the king of the crapper. I like the shitbox more than any man.*

In fact, he's so clear about his love for anal sex he's refused to continue dating women who don't share his passion. *At some point during sex, I try to jam the old Bonecrusher in her wishing well. If she moves away, I try to hit that rusty wheel hole again from a different angle. If she says she doesn't do that. Then I ask why not. Maybe she's never tried. If she still don't go for it. Bye-bye baby, bye-bye!*

Isn't it wrong to keep insisting on a sexual act when someone doesn't want to do it? *A professional like me does it with real skill, fella.*

If I'm really pounding and ripping on the pussy, I ain't stopping when there is a whole other landmark to visit. You've got to give the whole woman the attention she deserves!

Gary from Florida feels his experience busting the backdoor is worthy of recognition. If the sex industry ever invents an Ass Sex Hall of Fame, he's ready for his trophy. *Look fella, I already have an acceptance speech typed out. If any man deserves first-ballot status it's me!*

Recently, Gary revealed he had fallen in love. I thought this was some of the most shocking news he had ever shared since he's an avowed bachelor.

It happened at the point of death, fella. She made me go kayaking. I hated it. We were paddling along and fish started jumping out of the water. One hit me in the head. I thought I was going to die and I just blurted it out—I love you!

Some women may be upset that their man can only express intimate feelings at the point of death but Gary's girlfriend was okay with it. Maybe it's because she knows he's willing to make huge sacrifices for her.

The first time we had sex. I took several stabs at her shithole but she wasn't letting me in. She kept saying don't do it there, I want it in the front. I finally found the solution. When I'm bending her over the couch and her head is hanging down that is the front to me. I said, yeah darling I'm stabbing the front hole. She said, you can play with it, flick it, fondle it, finger it, but you ain't fucking it!

The ironic thing is that Gary's relationship with this girlfriend may work. Any man that's willing to sacrifice something this important for the sake of love has a shot at happiness. Nothing says love more than respecting someone's request to not get fucked in the ass.

Awful Facebook Rule #7: End with Horrible Hashtags

Using corny hashtags in your Facebook updates is more maddening than a Peyton Manning *Papa John's* commercial. Because of that, *End with Horrible Hashtags* is another great way to make Facebook awful.

Hashtags may serve a purpose.

If you're searching for comments on a topic. I don't use them and I don't give a fuck if my tweet doesn't wind up in that topic feed. I want no part of the corny hashtag community. If you're a grown man please stop using hashtags. Hashtags are for chicks like this woman in her god-awful post.

#LimeadeLoser

When you have middle-aged soccer moms using hashtags, you know it's time to get rid of them!

> When working long hours on any project a Sonic Limeade is a must have! #FamilyTradition, #ILikeMineWith #Strawberries #Rebel.

After reading this post I decided that I'd never use a hashtag again. I'm done with them!

There's no reason to type #Rebel. You're not a rebel because you drank a fucking limeade at Sonic. Suck the guy's dick that brought the limeade out to your car—that's rebellious! #Swallow

#CircleOfJerks

I can't believe this next one. It's a picture of nine guys standing together hugging on each other. Some of them have beards and look like hipster douchebags. The picture was posted with a black-and-white filter, which proves someone took time making this as perfect as possible. Then, over the picture they've embedded some text that reads:

> 🤠 #SleepBroOver

There is no way there wasn't a circle jerk at this sleepover!

Think about it. Nine guys. Three beds in a normal house. That's three guys to each bed. Let me guess, the guy sleeping in the middle, at some point in the night, pretended he was skiing. I'll leave it at that.

SleepBroOver! *How fucking horrible is that!?*

Wow, I feel sorry for women these days. I really do. These are the men that are out there for single women. I think Facebook posts like this have changed some female lives forever. There are women who have no gay tendencies and zero sexual desire for other women who have seen pictures like this and made a dramatic change in their lifestyle.

Yeah, my man told me he was having a SleepBroOver with eight other guys. So, I decided I'm just going to start eating pussy. I really don't want to because I love dick but it seems like my boyfriend likes dick more and is planning on a buffet of cocks this weekend. I should've known something was up with him when he started using hashtags on every social media post. I hope he enjoys his new lifestyle. #AtLeastIDon'tHaveToSwallowAnymore.

Is this why everyone is getting their parts cut off or new ones put on and going through gender reassignment? You can thank this circle of jerks for ruining a whole generation of women.

#FuckedByAFairyTale

A very excited chick posted this next one with her photo of a rainbow.

> ⛽ My baby and I are about to get in the car and go find the end of this rainbow! #EndOfTheRainbow #PotOfGold #ThePromise

Her baby is her boyfriend. Do you think that guy wants to go on this trip? I'd rather get in the car and drive off a cliff. I just hope he had enough balls to question her.

Honey, let's go get in the car and find the end of the rainbow!

What's going to be at the end of the rainbow? he asks. What do you think we are going to find?

Well, you know, the pot of gold that's at the end of the rainbow, she says.

Really? I watch the news and I've never seen a story about someone discovering a pot of gold.

Don't you think it will be fun to just drive until we find the end of the rainbow?

Maybe when I was five. Not now, NOT EVER!

Lady, I can save you a lot of time and gas. You know what's at the end of the rainbow—AN APPLEBEE'S!

#NoInkForMe

Here's another reason hashtags have to end. Read what this fucking guy wrote.

> 🔧 Just got my ass handed to me at the auto shop. Went in for an oil change left $500 less and depressed. LOL! There goes my tattoo appointment for tomorrow! Guess I can wait one more month.

First of all, he didn't laugh out loud. Anytime a mechanic comes out to the waiting room and gives you bad news like that you don't laugh out loud. That's the last thing you do. You're usually angry and sad.

Second, no one needs to know that you're getting your car repaired. Also, no one cares it costs $500. It always costs at least $500.

Lastly, maybe you should wait another month for that bad Chinese symbol tattoo you're going to get that you have no idea what it means. It will be meaningless to you in a few years like most tattoos are.

At first glance, this guy's post is like him: a worthless waste of space. But, oh shit, take cover; here comes the real message via some rapid-fire hashtags!

> \# #NoInkForMe #FeelLikePunchingThroats #BeerMeX5 #BrokeAgain #SellingMyAssThisWeekend #IOnlyNeedOneKidneyRight #WhoNeedsTwoLungs #HeadedToTheSpermBank #RaiseMyAss

Watch out everyone this guy means business!

#NoInkForMe #FeelLikePunchingThroats

Whose *throats* are you going to punch? The mechanic's? Remember you said you were laughing out loud like a teenage girl when you found out the price. If you're going to *punch any throats* it should be your parents for raising a kid that whines over a car repair.

#BrokeAgain #SellingMyAssThisWeekend

If you're serious about selling your ass this weekend, why don't you just find a gay mechanic and you two can work out some kind of deal. The only thing it will cost is your dignity.

#IOnlyNeedOneKidneyRight #WhoNeedsTwoLungs

We get it; you don't have the money for the repairs. How long are you going to hammer this point home?

#BeerMeX5

Wow, this guy really can't handle anything thrown his way. Beer me times five because of an unexpected car repair? What will happen to him later in life if he has to foreclose on his house? Heroin times fifty? I can only hope!

#DogParkDisaster

If you have a Facebook friend like this, please steal her pet and force her to get off Facebook before you give it back. She writes:

> People that bring their dog to the dog park but do not allow them to play with other dogs are confusing to me. Do you take your kid to the playground and say don't play with other kids? #PeopleUnclearOnTheConcept #YourPoorDog

Here's another fucking douche that proves there is no room for fucking hashtags. You already clearly explained yourself in your post. No need to repeat everything with hashtags. Everyone knows what a dog park is, they just don't want their dog near yours.

Dogs aren't like humans. They don't need to be friends with other strange dogs. They are close to the people who live in their home. That's all they need.

They're not depressed the next day if they can't hang out with the dog they met yesterday in the park. They don't exchange phone numbers or friend each other on Facebook.

Your dog doesn't care. He just wants to smell a few things, piss, shit, and go back home. A dog park is where lonely people meet because they don't know how to have a real relationship with a human so they have one through their pet. They probably don't have any kids and treat their dog like one.

People that go to a dog park do *understand the concept*. They just don't care for you or your dog. So mind your business, pick up your dog's shit, and be on your way. #Cunt

#ChargersDouchebag

Here's another fucking douche that proves there is no more room for these fucking hashtags. He posted a picture of his dumb fat face with his San Diego Chargers hat on and he has his fat fist in the camera. The guy that sent this to me wrote one thing in the email: *Freaking Homo!*

> **#** Guess who's game ready? #BoltUpBaby!
> #ComeGetSome #Representing #LoveMyTeam
> #MondayNightFootball #GameReady #Pow
> #LetsGoChargers #JustWin #SanDiegoChargers
> #WooRaa #FootballSelfie #SeeYa

Now, do you see why I hate these fucking hashtags?

Okay, fatso, how are you *game ready*? Let's break it down.

You posted a picture of yourself sitting on your couch. You're a blob who likes the Chargers. You have beer and chips in front of you. You have the remote right there and the TV is on. Does that mean you are game ready? Is someone going to walk in your house and say wow dude, you're game ready! What's gotten into you? Nobody is going to do that. Even if you have a wife, she wouldn't walk in the room and say, *I guess you are game ready, honey!* You weigh 400 pounds and you have bigger tits than your wife. You would never be capable of playing football. You may be food ready but not game ready! It's also a Monday night game. Wait until his shitty team is down 27-0 at halftime and he goes to bed and misses the second half because he has to work in the morning. I guess that means you quit on your team then.

#ComeGetSome

Come get what? What am I getting? I don't know what that means. Certainly not the food because you've already eaten it. How about I come get you and take you to the gym?

#Representing

I get it asshole you spent $200 on that jersey and another $30 on that hat. I realize you are representing. You are also an ass. Whatever fucking jersey you bought won't mean shit soon. That player will be off the team next year and you'll wonder what to do with that jersey. Good move, douche! You're representing a guy that will get cut or leave in free agency next year. I guess you can always use your jersey as a tarp.

#LoveMyTeam #MondayNightFootball

You really are a crazy fucker! You're nuts, man. Not many people love their team or watch *Monday Night Football*. Nope, you're the only one, aren't you fucking special. You really went out on a limb with that statement.

#GameReady

What a minute, you've mentioned being game ready TWICE! Maybe because you opened the beer and the bag of chips, so now you're hashtag game ready. Did you tape your ankles up to get game ready? How about taping the refrigerator closed and do some sit-ups.

#Pow

What are you, four years old and watching *Batman*? What the fuck do you mean by *Pow*? Maybe you refer to a girlfriend as a "prisoner of war" because she's trapped in a relationship with you and has to deal with your fucking nonsense!

#LetsGoChargers #JustWin

Really, you don't want them to tie or lose? You want them to win? If I walk into a place and see some fat fuck on a couch in a Chargers jersey and Chargers hat, I have a feeling he wants them to win. You don't have to write it or post it on Facebook. Everyone knows it. You are a grown man dressed like an ass, you don't have to tell us you want them to win. We get it, motherfucker! If you were sitting there in a fucking button-down and khakis and a Bluetooth in your ear maybe I wouldn't know.

#WooRaa

Is that a new sandwich you're about to eat? I don't know what that means and don't want to know.

#FootballSelfie

There you go, need I say more?

#SeeYa

See you where? I don't hang out in places you hang out. I don't want to see you. I'm sure most of your friends would rather not see you. But they can't help it because your big frame is always in their eyeline. I know they didn't want to see this stupid picture on their Facebook feed.

I do want to see one thing. I want to see you in fucking tears after the game when your fucking team gets destroyed.

#BestieTakedown

Here is a post I'm not annoyed with. I love what this chick wrote.

> Every time I see the word #Bestie, a little bit of vomit comes up in my throat. Grown-ass women of the world, please stop using it!

This could be the greatest post ever!

One woman wrote in the comments section, *Wow, someone woke up on the wrong side of the bed today.*

No, she didn't! She woke up and realized that she had enough of her middle-aged women friends using the same slang that twelve-year-old girls use. You're not twelve anymore. You're forty-six! A twelve-year-old is getting her first period soon and you're close to getting your last period.

NERD CAMP-OUTS

What's going on with the iPhone craze in this country? Why are people camping overnight for a fucking phone?

Remember when people camped overnight for Led Zeppelin tickets? That made sense. Waiting for a phone is absolutely stupid.

In a year, these phone nerds will be complaining their version sucks especially when a new one comes out with better features.

As I write this, Apple has released about fourteen different versions of the iPhone. That's fourteen different models sold in less than nine years! They keep upgrading it because they keep screwing it up! I don't care if there is an extra pixel in the fucking screen, give me an extra hour of battery life! That's what I really need!

These nerd campers are such a big deal they do TV news interviews. "This is a status symbol," they say. "I could be the first one of my friends to get this!"

I'd rather be the first one of my friends to get herpes, and I was!

One nerd said, "You know this has been a roller coaster of emotion out here waiting in line."

NO IT HASN'T! You're on a roller coaster of emotion when you lose a family member—not standing in line talking about the latest *Big Bang Theory* episode.

Thank goodness the latest superhero movie didn't open at the same time. What line would these nerds get in? *Oh, my God, it's the new Superman movie or the new iPhone, where should we sleep?*

None of these guys are getting laid. They are all nerds. They don't get pussy on a regular basis and that's not going to change.

Girls are not impressed that you have the latest iPhone. I've never heard a woman say, "Wow, is that the new iPhone? That's hot! Let me give you a blow job!"

If that was the case I would've camped out a month ago!

Awful Facebook Rule #8:
Challenge Us Like Chumps

This section details the excruciatingly stupid challenges Facebook idiots force on us. A terrible trend that doesn't seem to have an end in sight. I don't want to play games with you. Stop posting your bullshit games on my wall.

Most challenges are brutally stupid, waste our time, and always find a way to draw attention to the person who posted it. I don't have to belabor the point, just read the next example and you'll see why *Awful Facebook Rule #8* is *Challenge Us Like Chumps*.

The Warm Goo Challenge

This challenge is from a woman who seems to love the sensation of warm goo deep in her body. Good for the guy she's married to but bad for everyone else.

> October goosies challenge!

That phrase is more cringe-worthy than an ISIS beheading video.

Her next post is an attempt to define her stupid, made-up word *goosies*. Jesus, I hate even writing that word.

> A feeling of warm ooey-gooeyness inside, happiness generating throughout the entire body, sometimes causing a tingling sensation, and usually caused by simple pleasures. Now, write the top three things in your life that gives you goosies. Go! All of you! Don't make me tag you.

First, I despise when someone writes, *Go!* There's no reason for that. Everybody understands your pathetic game. If you leave out the word go, it's not going to confuse your friends. No one will say, *I wanted to take part in your little game but you didn't write go. I even kept refreshing the page waiting for your signal to start. It never popped up so I gave up on it!*

Just to prove my point, I'll play the game right now. Here are my top three things that give me the *goosies*:

1. Blow jobs
2. Blumpkins
3. Ass-to-mouth

How's that for *goosies*? Now, GO do it! Do I have any takers?

The Fuck Along Challenge

Read this guy's brutally lame challenge. It's embarrassing!

> ✈ So next Friday the family and I are going to go on a little trip. There are a few of you that know where we are going so I just ask that you please don't post where we are going. I thought it would be kinda cool to post some pictures along the way to try and see if anyone can figure out where we are going. If you feel like playing along just leave a comment here and this is where I will post the pictures when it's time!

I would love to see the pictures of you getting ready for that trip. In fact, everybody you know on Facebook would be interested in that. Here's what you should do.

First Clue: Post a picture of your HIV negative test. That's a fascinating way to start!

Second Clue: Post a photo of you at the drugstore buying condoms and lube.

Third Clue: This should be a picture of a Viagra bottle and a picture of your wife doing Kegel exercises. That is going to make it fucking interesting!

Fourth Clue: When you get to the orgy house take a group picture of everyone before they take their clothes off.

Fifth Clue: The next picture is all the clothes lying on the floor. That's a fucking good clue. Something I would follow. It's a bit of a tease but people will beg you for the next clue.

Sixth Clue: The final image is one of an ice pack resting on your wife's snatch. She's holding it there because she took too many dicks.

The Breakfast Bitch Challenge

I wish I had the free time this next woman seems to have.

> 🍚 Should I have a smoothie or oatmeal for breakfast? I expect an answer when I get back!

I'm picturing her doing this early in the morning. She's out of the shower, getting dressed, trying to get ready for work. Typical morning routine everyone has.

Right at the point of eating some breakfast, she stops, grabs her phone, and challenges her Facebook friends with this question. Who gives a fuck what you eat? This woman is obviously begging for attention.

I guess she's thinking, *I don't get a lot of comments on my posts so I'll lure my friends in with this question. The last four or five posts got nothing so I'll leave it up to them then maybe they will say something.*

She's forcing her friends to respond. She tells them she expects an answer when she gets back!

Think about all of her friends and what they are doing in the morning. Let's imagine one of her girlfriends sees this. Let's say it's a woman with a few kids. She's trying to make sandwiches for their lunch boxes. One kid is tugging on her leg wanting more juice. The others are running around crazy looking for their books and school stuff.

This friend stops for a moment to check her phone and she sees this Facebook notification, reads this breakfast challenge, and thinks, *Oh man, she expects me to answer this question? I don't have time to help this stupid bitch pick what she's going to eat.*

I can imagine her checking back after about ten minutes and no one has responded. How depressing and pathetic will that be for her? She'll think, *This is fucked up! None of my friends give a shit about me. Did I make someone mad? Did I piss off all my friends?*

All of this shit goes through her head and this is the start of her day. Not to mention, she's spreading her negative mood to everyone else that reads this and feels annoyed about being imposed upon.

Thank God, in this case, one guy responded. But let's be honest, he's only doing it because he wants to bang her. Why the fuck else would someone respond to this stupid shit?

He writes, *Oatmeal!*

Oatmeal it is, she writes back.

Woohoo! I directly affected someone's life today.

Hahahahaha!

I'm glad you picked that because it was chilly and I would have been an icicle with the smoothie.

You wouldn't have been cold because you had a smoothie. Even if it's December, you're not drinking it in the backyard.

That factored into the equation! he writes back.

I give the guy a pass because I know what he's doing. This woman appears to be a decently hot chick. He noticed no one responded and thought if *I respond, I'll score a few points with her*. He's thinking, *this will help me get in her pants one day*. He didn't give a fuck if she ate a smoothie or oatmeal he just wants to eat her ass!

The Shut Up & Die Challenge

> OK, ladies and gentlemen, time to play. When you think of me, what is the first song that pops into your head? Be honest. I just want to know what it is.

All right sir, I don't know you, but these are the three songs that pop into my head after reading your terrible challenge:

1. *Die Mother Fucker Die* by Dope
2. *People = Shit* by Slipknot
3. *I Want Bad Things to Happen to You* by Wednesday 13

The Fuck My Friend Challenge

I'm single again and back on the dating scene, but women like the next one make me question what the hell I'm getting into.

> Going forward if anyone else happens to post on my wall. I would like to know your favorite song from a movie soundtrack for funzies! I'll get things started I have two: "You Don't Own Me" from the First Wives Club and "Cause I'm a Blonde" from the Earth Girls Are Easy soundtrack.

Is that what I have to deal with in the dating world?

If any woman likes *First Wives Club* she hates men. That's a big man-hating movie. The only reason I know this is because my ex-father-in-law would watch it all the time. When we visited his house it was always on in the background. I was going to divorce his daughter over that but then I caught her having an affair with a twenty-two-year-old college student that still lives at home. That made my decision easier. Isn't that *funzies*?

If I start dating a girl and she says, *Hey, do you want to have sex with me and my girlfriend?*

Are you fucking serious?

Well, yeah, for funzies!

NOPE!

Why? Aren't you attracted to my friend?

Yes, but you said that awful word. So, now I'm going to have a little funzies with myself and my hand.

The Last Challenge Challenge

Guess this next challenge was created by a whole group of friends on Facebook. One of them started this song lyric game and the rest kept it going. Talk about *funzies*, this is the definition of *funzies*! I'd rather participate in a NAMBLA meeting.

> ↳ This is the game. I'll start it off. What if Bruno Mars wasn't your man? Keep it going!

Here are the responses to his post:

What if Lil John didn't Turn Down for What? Keep it going!

What if Madonna wasn't a Material Girl? Keep it going!

What if it didn't feel good to be a gangster? Keep it going!

What if Dolly Parton worked 8 to 4?

What if Prince drove a little red Volkswagen and wore a raspberry baseball cap?

What if the Beatles needed more than love?

What if Otis Redding jumped off the Dock of the Bay?

What if the Fresh Prince's parents were understanding?

What if Fat Bottomed Girls didn't make the Rockin' World Go Round?

What if Afroman never got high?

What if Rick Springfield actually had Jessie's Girl?

What if 867-5309 actually had a Jenny?

What if I ended the chapter here? You can put the book down a moment and reflect on how thankful you are that you didn't participate in this game.

CHAPTER SEVEN

CRANK YANKERS: THE EARLY YEARS

Six months after Howard Stern played my prank calls, a new opportunity presented itself that took my career in an unexpected direction. Jimmy Kimmel and Adam Carolla were coming off a successful run on *The Man Show* at Comedy Central and wanted to do a new television show that would present their brand of comedy in a whole new light. Like Howard Stern, Jimmy Kimmel was a huge fan of prank calls.

Kimmel had heard about me through *The Howard Stern Show* and tracked me down, and I was offered the job. Professional comedians would record prank phone calls, like what I had done on *Terrorizing Telemarketers*, and the calls would be dramatized with puppets and animation.

When I was first pitched on the idea, I thought the whole concept was awful; especially when they told me the show would use puppets. I figured it would last about three episodes before the suits running the network realized it was a disaster and cancelled the whole thing. *Crank Yankers* launched in 2002 and ended up running until 2005. It was revived a few years later on MTV2 in 2007.

Welcome to Yankerville

Many fans of the show wondered how it was put together. The most common question was how do you work the puppet and do the voice at the same time. I never worked the puppets and thank God, I didn't. I've had my hand up someone's ass before but never a puppet.

My routine on the show was very easy. I did the voice of the character, recorded the call in the studio, and left to go get drunk. That was it for my part. They would fly us first-class to Las Vegas and put us up in the Four Seasons hotel to make prank phone calls. God Bless America.

The Rebirth of the Retard

Eventually, two of the characters I voiced, Special Ed and Bobby Fletcher, became favorites on the show. The writers transformed the character I simply called Retard into Special Ed. They had to change the name to something more politically correct and I had to sign ownership of the character over to Comedy Central for free. They wanted to own the character outright, if I said no, they would just find another person for the show. I figured let them have it; I'll come up with something else down the road that I can own. It was either continue telling jokes in shitty bars or get exposure on a national television show.

My mother would only watch the Special Ed segments because she's very religious.

She said, "I want to tell my friends that you're on a TV show but you play a retarded kid with a helmet! I can't tell my church friends that!"

My mom was really proud that I was on the show but was praying for me because she thought doing this character might hurt my chances for getting into heaven someday. Meanwhile, if she went in my room and saw the fifty-gallon drum of hand cream she would realize I was a long shot to make it.

Crank Yankers was well received and eventually developed a cult following, but the first year of the show had relatively low ratings. However, it had its fans and many of them were celebrities. During the *2003 MTV Movie Awards*, Eminem won for Best Male Performance in a Movie. He wasn't at the show that year so he submitted a video clip thanking MTV for the honor. The entire segment was Eminem doing an impression of Special Ed. A salute to his favorite show—*Crank Yankers*.

Shortly after that, I got word that Eminem was interested in doing a skit on *Crank Yankers* and he wanted it to be with one of my characters. Apparently, Eminem had a soft spot for the show because he watched it with his daughter. The two of them had a routine of imitating their favorite character, Special Ed. So, the producers decided that they would send me out to Detroit to meet with Eminem. The plan was that we would spend a day recording different calls at his studio.

I was so excited to fly out to Detroit that I didn't pay attention to what I was packing in my luggage. I had a couple of boxes of stink bombs in my travel bag.

If you've never seen them, stink bombs are tiny glass tubes you throw down to the ground and step on. When they break open, they release a sulfur-like substance that produces a horrible smell like rotten eggs. Some of my comedian friends and I were notorious for dropping these stink bombs at the most random times.

For instance, Jim Norton and I would go to the local dance club and prank people with these little vials. We would be in different corners of a room and drop them simultaneously and then people would go nuts trying to get away from it. It would clear the dance floor in seconds. We were stink-bomb terrorists and nobody was sure when we would strike next.

As I was going through security at the airport they found the stink bombs in my bag. They asked me to step out of line and eventually took me into one of the back rooms for questioning.

"What is this?" They asked me. "Are you trying to bring a controlled substance onto the airplane?"

I looked around the room. There were three cops, two senior TSA guys, and an immature comedian in the middle. It was a bad scene. I tried to explain what it really was. One of the cops grabbed my driver's license and wanted to know what I was up to.

I said, "I'm a comic and when I travel me and my comedian friends will drop these stink bombs in crowded areas and watch people run for cover. They smell like farts. It's really funny." Everyone was just staring at me in disgust when the cop holding my license blurted out, "You are thirty-three years old, what the fuck is wrong with you?"

Now I'm panicking because I think I'm going to miss my flight so I say, "You see, I'm flying to Detroit for this television show called *Crank Yankers.*"

One officer perked up.

"Really, I've seen that show! Comedy Central, right?"

"Yeah, that's it. I do some of the characters on that show."

"Oh yeah, which ones?" He asked.

"Well, there's Special Ed for one," I said.

"NO WAY! You do Special Ed? Do it for me!"

I cleared my throat and conjured up the retard.

"Yaaaaaaaaaaaayyyyyyy!"

The cop laughed. "Yep, that's it! Okay, get the fuck out of here. You have about five minutes to get on that plane. GO!"

So, I grabbed my bag, ran to the gate, and thankfully caught the plane to Detroit. If you ever wonder why we still have issues with security at airports this story illustrates the problem. All you have to do to bypass our national security is imitate Special Ed's stupid voice!

Meeting Eminem

Once I made it to Detroit, I was nervous about meeting Eminem because if he doesn't like you he will write a whole album about you. I didn't want to be public enemy #1. But, once we were introduced, I realized I had nothing to worry about.

"I can't believe I'm in the room with Special Ed!" He said as he walked into the studio and shook my hand.

"Likewise, great to meet you," I said.

In no time, we were recording prank calls where I was Special Ed and he was Special Em, and one call we made was to a 99 cents store asking how much products were over and over again until the staff people couldn't take it anymore and hung up on us. We kept at it for about six hours and then went out to dinner. For months after that, I would periodically get crank calls from Special Em. Of course, I recognized Eminem immediately but I would play dumb and go along with him because if I called him out he would stop calling me. I let him continue doing it for at least a year pretending I had no idea who it was. A year later he and I did a bit on the *MTV Video Music Awards* where he beats up Special Ed onstage. I was amazed that Special Ed had grown popular enough that he could be a presenter on a major award show. To think it all started with me doing that terrible voice in my dingy apartment back in Jersey. I had no idea it would come to this.

Crank Yankers lasted for four seasons and lived on in reruns. It was a great gig for me. You might say it was the American dream come true—burping and acting like a retard while paying off a mortgage—God Bless America!

Awful Facebook Rule #9:
Post a Worthless Weather Update

The fastest way to get me to delete you on Facebook is to post a worthless weather update. There are so many of these on social media it's like a bad joke plague.

If you know someone following Rule #9 please lure them into the next lightning storm and make sure they are electrocuted. Just read the following examples and you'll see how fast innocent small talk about the weather can ruin your day!

Fighting the Seasons

Winter's Bone

This fuck wants to fight winter because he's annoyed with the colder temperatures.

> If this winter was a man, I would kick him in the dick repeatedly and tell him, "Thanks for ruining all our fun!"

Are you really going to kick winter in the dick? I'm just curious how that's physically possible? How do you know winter is a man? If winter is a woman are you going to kick her repeatedly in the cunt?

Let's accept that winter is a real person. How will you find him and give him this beating? Will you drive around in your car looking for winter? Maybe you'll hire a private investigator?

Let's say you see winter at a Ruby Tuesday's hanging out with his family, summer, spring, and fall. Will you wait until he finishes his potato skins before you assault him? Aren't you worried summer, spring, and fall might jump in and stop the fight? Hmmm, I don't think you've thought this through very well!

Unless you ski, the winter usually sucks for people. You might want to think about relocating to a warmer state. I have a gut feeling that winter is going to be around for a long time. But, if you get in touch with winter, can you tell him not to let it snow on my property because I'm sick of shoveling snow. My neighbors will think it's strange when they are snowed in and my house and driveway are bone dry but I'll just tell them about you.

Yeah, there was a guy on Facebook that kicked winter in the dick. He told winter not to snow on my house!

If I knew who posted this, I would find him and kick him repeatedly in the dick. But, then again, he's bitching about the weather on Facebook—that probably means he has a cunt.

Crazy Dies Hard

There's no reason for this post.

> Whoever wished it would cool down a bit because they were a little hot. I'm pretty sure the genie from the lamp you found answered your wish. Way to waste one of your three wishes on garbage. Thanks for ending the summer early asshole.

I'm curious where you find a genie in a bottle? A garage sale? On a beach? An antique store? How does this guy know that this is one of the wishes requested? Don't you think a guy with a genie would wish for a bigger dick before he'd change the weather?

Let's say someone did find a real genie in a bottle. No one is going to make wishes about changing the weather. My three wishes would be to end terrorism, ban this fuck from Facebook, and to pull a threesome—in no particular order.

What's strange is he posted this in the middle of September, the traditional time that the weather cools down. A few minutes later, he flips to the other extreme.

> It is definitely a beautiful day out today. It feels like it is mid-fall but the trees and flowers still look midsummer. That's a pretty darn good day! It's the simple things in life that is given to us day in and day out that we must not forget to enjoy.

This motherfucker is truly bipolar. One minute ago, he was ready to kill the guy who had wished for cooler weather. Now he's writing a fucking Hallmark card about how wonderful the weather is and preaching to all of his Facebook friends about how they need to enjoy the simpler things in life.

He goes from hating the new season and wanting to murder a genie to loving the change in weather. Guess what, he's not done!

His next post takes another unexpected turn and confirms he's nuts:

 I just had a dream I played the role of John McClane in Die Hard. Eat your heart out Bruce Willis! I played the role perfect.

Do you think someone sent this over to Bruce Willis? Do you think it ruined his day? I bet Bruce took a moment to think about his career after reading this.

Fuck man, this guy played the role perfect! Maybe I should get in contact with him and find out what the hell he did to play it so perfect. Maybe he could coach me on how to be a better actor?

I've never heard anyone complain that Bruce Willis was bad in that role. It doesn't seem like this shithead is enjoying *the simple things in life* if he's dreaming about replacing an actor in a movie from 1988. Will his next post say he's mad that the senior George Bush won the election?

Bruce Willis and *Die Hard* haven't been in the news for ages. What would possess this guy to make this post? Hey dude, do everyone a favor and use that *genie from the lamp* to wish for an early death.

Harassing the Weather

Noah's Douche Ark

Here is another douchebag complaining about the weather.

> ☂   Yowza! It is pouring outside. Call Noah!

Does Noah have a phone? It's been about 5,000 years since we heard from Noah.

Also, does this guy think Noah can build an ark that quick? If the rain is already *"pouring outside"* isn't it too late?

Never mind the timing, I understand why this guy posted this. There's been a bunch of reports about Noah showing up and building a quick ark and saving families and pets from drowning, right? What? No? You don't recall that happening? You know why, because it never did!

I hope someone floods this guy's Facebook page with kiddie porn!

Pissing on Storm Gods

This guy writes:

> ❄   The storm gods must be really messed up in the heavens today. We have really heavy snow that is coming down like rain and now crazy thunder. Either they are getting it on up there or throwing up after a morning of partying.

There are no storm gods in heaven and if there were, they're certainly not drinking or fucking. I don't think God is going to let people get shitfaced or have sex in heaven. He won't let a storm of cum and puke fall from the skies onto innocent people.

If God did let the storm gods drink, he wouldn't let them do it in the morning. Maybe he would let them have a cocktail before bed. What kind of example would he be setting if he let people get drunk in the morning?

I hate when people say, *He's up in heaven drinking a beer.*

No, he's not. Where would he get the alcohol? Is there a liquor store up there? You'd think a liquor salesman would have talked about making deliveries to heaven, right? If there is how does the liquor get delivered? By airplane? What airline flies to heaven? I just checked United and the furthest they go is Australia. I want to know. I could use the frequent flyer miles.

Your friend isn't drinking in heaven. He's in a wooden box in the ground. Stop thinking like a child.

Why are you saying the storm gods are fucking because the *heavy snow is coming down like rain and now crazy thunder*? They wouldn't multitask while they're having sex. I highly doubt a female storm god is going to interrupt the male god while he's eating her pussy, just to make some heavy snow and thunder. Anyway, if the storm gods were really fucking wouldn't the snow be sticky and chunky?

GARY FROM FLORIDA: SHIRTS & SQUIRTERS

Gary from Florida is so committed to getting laid that he purchased a liquor store for about $400,000 just so he could meet more women. He didn't go into this lightly. He had every intention to make sure it was profitable, which it was, but the main goal was to fuck as many women as possible in the cooler in the back of the store. Something about sex at thirty-four degrees Fahrenheit makes Gary hot. Why? He's *Gary from Florida*, that's why!

Gary tells me while he owned the store he only pursued a small fraction of the women he met. *Out of hundreds of numbers there were about twenty women worth calling. I ended up banging about six chicks in that cooler. It was easy, I'd call them up, take them out for dinner, tell them lets go back to my place, I know a guy that owns a liquor store. They'd always say, yeah, I bet you do! We'd laugh and stop at the store for some booze.*

Lights, Camera, Cooler!

Some people might think Gary will bang any woman willing to bend over but for the cooler he wanted a pro for what he had in mind. His dream finally came true when a hot porno star started frequenting his store.

I saw this very beautiful girl in my store. She gave me her phone number and I found out from a friend she was an ex-porno star. I asked her out and she came by the store around midnight at closing. She was dressed in all black looking beautiful. She had been drinking, so we went in the cooler and did more vodka shots. We kissed and the next thing you know I was fucking her in the crapper. She even did ass-to-mouth, fella! I shot my seed down her throat and then again on one of her ass cheeks. She loved it so much she said I should be in one of her movies!

When I ask Gary if he thought he should have worn a condom he said, *If I'm going to die might as well go out banging one of the top porno stars in America! That sex was so good, I went home and whacked my bag afterwards!*

Bed of Hennessy

Gary loved having sex in the back of the store and he made a special bed for that purpose. *Yes sir, fella. I got a shipment of about $60,000 in Hennessy one time and stacked it in a ten-by-ten shape. It was about three feet off the ground. I even formed a headboard so it looked like a bed.*

When one of his favorite taste-testing girls scheduled to work his store, he felt confident he would get a chance to use it. *Taste test girls come in the store all the time. They're hot young women that dress sexy and offer small sips of a product. They make about $30 per hour and clear over a hundred a shift. This one I knew. She was thirty-four* *and super hot. During her breaks, we would go in the back and do Jägerbombs. After her shift was over, and we had done the fourth or fifth Jägerbomb, I kissed her and squeezed her tits. I laid her out on that bed of Hennessy and took her panties off. She had this beautiful pure black pussy hair. I ate her box until my cock was standing straight like a flag- pole. Then we fucked on the Hennessy bed for about an hour. It was awe- some, fella! She came all over my six and a sixteenth mule!*

Pussy Power Wash

Gary from Florida's most memorable night in the liquor store produced a sacred piece of history that is now preserved in his hall of fame memorabilia.

I met this woman online and after one of our dates we went to my store to get a couple of bottles of wine. We went in the cooler and I got horny and put her up on that bed of Hennessy to eat her box. She stopped me right as I was about to give her the motorboat. She warned me she was a squirter. I said no problem not knowing how serious she was about her condition. I should have put a mask and snorkel on, fella!

When she started spraying, it was like getting my teeth cleaned with a power washer. Later when I was fucking her, she sprayed again and it was so forceful it pushed my cock out of her box. When it was all said and done, I looked down and saw that my shirt and pants were covered. That sucked because I had my most expensive shirt on that night and my best pants. I never did get the stain out. Now I keep that shirt in my closet, like Monica Lewinsky's dress, it's a fucking souvenir, fella! Hall of fame material—no doubt about it!

Awful Facebook Rule #10:
Drown Us in Dumb-ass Details

In church you're taught that God cares about you so much that he knows your every thought, and wants you to talk to him all day long.

I'm horrified to say, that many people treat Facebook as if it was God or an imaginary friend.

They post updates all day pretending Facebook cares what they say. They share every fucking thought that comes to their mind. Even if it's an incomplete idea or random nonsense. Here are a few examples.

Zika Please!

A guy posted this:

> Just killed a mosquito.

I hope it bit you before you killed it and it had malaria!

Prick with Purpose

Another guy posted this:

> Is it me or is it my sole purpose in life to troll Facebook during my free time at work?

It's you!

Shit Sauce

A woman posted this:

> I just got six jars of Prego Sauce for $0.83 cents each!

WHO GIVES A FUCK?!

Not in Heat

A dumb-ass woman posted this:

> I just love having a dog who loves the cold. Wait, what did I say?

Look lady, you know exactly what you said. You read that status update to make sure the spelling and grammar was correct before you posted it. You should only worry about *what did I just say* if your last update said, *I just sucked off my dog!*

Shit-Stains with Wipers

It pains me to write this next one.

> Yea! My windshield wipers won't turn off! Fantastic!

This guy wants people to feel sorry for him over a problem that takes two minutes and $20 to fix. Imagine the crisis he's going to have if one day if his oil light goes on? What about when he needs new brakes? Holy shit, he'll have to go on antidepressants. Also, he wrote this in his car while he was driving. He risked running over a kid to let his four hundred friends know about his hardship. One guy commented:

> And mine won't turn on! Don't we make a pair!

You're lying. Your wipers turn on. You wouldn't be driving around if your wipers didn't work. That's something that gets fixed immediately. You guys do actually make a pair—a pair of zilches!

Hair Are Two Idiots

Have you noticed how a lot of people post about work they need to do instead of doing it?

> 😀 So much dog hair to vacuum up. I don't know how it accumulates so fast.

Sir, what happens is hair falls off the dog and onto the floor because some dogs shed more than others. Does that make fucking sense? Maybe you don't clean it up everyday and that's why it's all over the place.

His friend comments:

> 🐺 I know what you mean dude, my dog sheds a lot too.

Wow, fucking fascinating. I hope the next post this guy writes is, "The hair on my head is falling out at an alarming rate. I don't know how it accumulates so fast." I would click on the like button the second I saw the post.

Boob Bozo

Read this Facebook update and see if you can guess the age of the person posting it.

> 😊 It's that time of year again to be thankful. This year I choose to be grateful for BOOBIES because no matter what size they are they make you smile!

A forty-year-old man wrote this. My five-year-old son doesn't even say the word *boobies* anymore. He's already calling them tits. This guy obviously hasn't seen a lot of them because they all don't make you smile. I've ended up with a frown on my face many times after getting a girl's shirt off. Some tits are flat, or droopy, or covered in stretch marks. Those make me well up with tears!

Why are you grateful this year? Tits aren't seasonal like pumpkin beer. He should take a look at my ninety-year-old grandmother's rack. Would that make him smile? All I know is he'll have to call a friend to help him lift those tits back into her bra!

Sunday Assault

A guy posts:

> Grab me a chunk of Sunday. If you grab too much, share it.

If a chick wrote this I wouldn't even make fun of it but this is a dude? Where would I go to grab a chunk of Sunday? How about I grab a chunk of your wife's fat ass and share it with my six friends?

Why?

A fifty-year-old man posted this:

> Sometimes you feel like a nut, sometimes you don't!

This is a 1970s Almond Joy and Mounds candy bar jingle. The comments from his friends are really smart and riveting:

I remember that commercial!
Now, I feel like eating a candy bar!
I used to love Almond Joy's
No way, Mounds were way better!

Fucking fascinating!

FANTASY FOOTBALL NERDS

I'm in a sports bar watching football and fantasy football dorks are everywhere—guys with their laptops lined up on the bar and the tables. Why in the fuck would you bring your laptop to a sports bar?

I'm writing this during week four of the season. It isn't the last week of the season when you might expect guys needing to have instant information about the games. The season has just started. You don't need to know whether you won right away. Wait until you get home to check your team's stats.

I've had these dorks coming to me asking who just scored a touchdown. I ask, *Why do you want to know?*

Because of my fantasy football team!

My response is: *None of your business, none of your FUCKING BUSINESS!*

I heard one fantasy football guy saying, *I met a player that's on my roster. I went up to him and said, hey man I really like you. I have you on my fantasy football team!*

I told that guy just tell the player you think about him when you MASTURBATE! That's what you're really saying!

That NFL player isn't impressed with you. He thinks you're a creep. He doesn't care if you have him on your fantasy football team. He doesn't give a FUCK about you!

Stop it with these laptops in the sports bars.

But, I gotta check my stats, they say.

Why don't you check your pants for a PENIS!

Awful Facebook Rule #11:
Create a Shit Storm of Oversharing

This is the last rule in my list of *How to Make Facebook Awful* and it's the most horrifying example of this shit site: the oversharing.

That's right, think of the most personal things you can and post them on your Facebook page.

For instance, is your wife having hemorrhoid surgery? Share a few pictures of her nasty ass and tag the surgeon in your post. Is your niece getting her period? Show the evidence to all of your friends! Did your aunt die in a fire? Post a few pictures of her crispy corpse.

The Whiny Wino

Oversharing starts with the small things. Like this woman letting everyone in the world know, she's a hopeless alcoholic.

> 🍷 Wish I had an IV rather than a glass of wine, but this will have to do.

That's a great thing to share with people on Facebook. She's probably friends with her boss or people at work that don't like her. It's good for them to know when you're showing up late hung-over and asking for an aspirin every day.

Just drink a few glasses of wine and pass out. In the morning, be glad you didn't wake up next to Bill Cosby.

The Laxative Lady

Check out this next woman, who thinks we care about her shit—*literally*!

> Man, I'm tired. I'm lucky if I slept an hour through the night. It's my own fault. I wasn't going to the bathroom, as I should. So I decided to take two laxatives in the early afternoon. So, I still didn't go. I was worried that I was still backed up. It feels like my stomach was pushed to one side. So, I didn't go and before bed I took two more. Well . . . wrong thing to do! I have never gone to the bathroom so much. I'm lucky if I slept an hour. Won't do that again! So, needless to say my stomach is going crazy. Hey, at least it came out! Sorry about all the details!

That's a Facebook post from a chick! *Let that sink in.*

She says, *Sorry about all the details!*

Why are you apologizing? If you were really sorry about all the details, you would have edited this down. You're not really sorry, so stop lying. You intended to write all of this hoping everyone would feel bad for you. There's not one fucking ounce of you that's sorry. You planned every word and posted it exactly like you wanted it.

Her main point is that she was up all night *shitting.*

Wow, that's awesome!

Imagine if she was dating a guy who looked her up on Facebook. He would realize she is going to sit on the bowl all night and not on his face!

Mickey Mouse Shitter

Not all oversharing is personal. This woman loves to embarrass her son.

> This is how you poop at Disneyland!

She writes that, and then posts a picture of her kid taking a shit.

He's wearing Mickey Mouse ears and sitting on a toilet bowl in a stall with his pants down around his ankles. The poor kid is looking up at the camera and he has a big frown on his face. He looks like he hates his fucking mother for doing this. Wonder why? Now this is out there. Other kids will see this and make fun of him.

Hahaha, we saw the picture your mother posted on Facebook with your stupid Mickey Mouse ears and your pants down!

I hope the kid says:

Yeah, well, I was taking a shit and didn't know that my ATTENTION WHORE MOM would post that on Facebook for all of her friends to see.

Map to Ms. Asshole

Here's another mom exposing the personal details of her child's life.

> My poor baby had a bad asthma attack!

Instead of sending a text to a few close family members, she thinks it's a good idea to let her three hundred Facebook friends know that she's at the emergency room at the local hospital.

She's also tagged the hospital on the map on her page. Why do your friends need to have the exact location of the ER? No one is coming there to meet you. No one.

This woman posted this within two minutes of stepping into the hospital. Her kid is hyperventilating and may die but she thinks the real emergency is updating her Facebook page.

But, wait she's not done. A few posts later, she writes:

> *Saying goodbye to the beautiful angel.*

Guess where she is now? A funeral. HOLY SHIT!

Do you think everyone needs to know you are at a funeral?

I want to congratulate the guy who sent me this. He had the balls to write back to her.

On the hospital post he wrote:

> When I'm sick and need emergency attention the last thing I need is some attention from Facebook. That's the last thing on my mind.

YES!!! GOOD FOR YOU, SIR!

On the funeral post, he commented:

> Why would you post this when the person is already dead? Do you think they are going to click the like button?

You think this woman wants people to feel bad for her with these posts? She posts about her kid being sick and going to a funeral. The post in-between these two was an inspirational quote: *Live. Love. Laugh.* It doesn't seem like she's doing any of those things. It's more like she's bitching, bellyaching, and begging for attention.

Cool, Grandpa Is Dead!

Here is another shocking example of oversharing. This woman posts a simple message with a whole series of photos. Here's the update:

> My grandfather has died.

If I were friends with this woman I would click the like button on this post and then in the comments section write, "Good! One less old fuck driving on the road now!" I'd say that's a good way to get unfriended.

But, this woman takes it even further by tagging the location of the funeral home in her Facebook feed. Then, she shares:

Picture #1: Funeral flowers.

Picture #2: Coffin.

Picture #3: Coffin at the gravesite.

Picture #4: People crying at the funeral.

I have questions about these pictures.

Question #1: Which gas station sold you those shitty flowers?

Question #2: You think there is room in there for you, too?

Question #3: Nice shovel! Did you dig the grave yourself?

Question #4: When did you guys turn into a bunch of pussies?

Awww . . . What a Cute Corpse!

Just when I thought I had seen the worst possible funeral post, this one takes it to a whole other level of wrong. I guess dying grandfathers are a trend on Facebook now.

Picture #1: Grandfather on his deathbed. The old man is sleeping. Tubes run out of arms and nose into various machines. His awful grandchild has staged a photo by sitting on the bed beside this poor dying man. The kid has an over-exaggerated frown on his face as if to say, *Awww, poor old granddad!*

Picture #2: Grandfather has passed on. He posts a picture of the man lying dead on his hospital bed.

Picture #3: He takes a picture of himself at the wake.

Picture #4: He takes a picture of himself smiling next to an enlarged photo of his now dead grandfather.

Picture #5: Pallbearers carrying the coffin to the gravesite.

Picture #6: Coffin being lowered into the ground.

You know he had the person take a few shots so he can pick out the best one. That's the sickest part of this whole thing. The guy staged a photo shoot at his grandfather's funeral. I wish he would have handed me his phone to take the pictures at the gravesite. I would have told him to stand near the edge of the hole and keep backing up until he falls into it.

AWFUL CONVERSATIONS

CHAPTER EIGHT

CRAZY CONCERT STORIES

After the success of *Crank Yankers*, other opportunities in television started coming my way. I'm a heavy metal fan so when *That Metal Show* came along I jumped at the chance. The show was billed as the *Tonight Show* for AC/DC fans and was hosted by my good friends Eddie Trunk and Don Jamieson.

My introduction to heavy metal was as hard as the music itself. My older brothers forced it on me. From twelve to fourteen, they blasted me with their favorite heavy metal songs while they schlepped me around town. At fifteen, they took me to my first concert at Madison Square Garden. It was a double-bill with Black Sabbath and Van Halen and it was fucking fantastic! I started building my own collection of music after that.

As much as I loved the music, being a heavy metal kid in my school was rough. Most of the guys my age didn't know who the fuck Judas Priest was and the girls didn't give a shit. When I showed up at a house party wearing my best clothes, jeans and a *Blizzard of Ozz* shirt, no one would talk to me.

"Can you believe Slayer is fighting?" I'd say, giving it my best shot. "The band might break up!" The hot girls just stared at me like I was a total freak.

It was rare for girls to come to these heavy metal shows. The ones that did show up were hard on the eyes; the members of Slayer were better looking. I guess that explains why I was a virgin through high school. My room was filled with posters of heavy metal dudes and pro wrestlers. I stared at them for hours at a time. It's a miracle to this day that I never had a cock in my ass.

Fuck You, Scorpions!

One memorable night my luck changed. I drove to Philadelphia to see the Scorpions and met this hot chick at the show. We hit it off instantly. I had a floor ticket and somehow I got her down there with me. We pushed closer to the stage while the opening band played. She was super hot so the crowd let us through until we ended up in the front row.

I was nineteen at the time. I couldn't believe my luck! Imagine the perfect rock chick, Stacey was it. She was incredibly gorgeous and she had these huge, perfect tits stacked high in her tight T-shirt. We immediately started making out. In my head I was thinking, *I'm getting laid tonight, no question about it!*

Stacey was a big Scorpions fan so when they hit the stage she was really excited. Likewise, when the band noticed her they were excited, too. We kept making out and the band kept rocking. Stacey was in such a good mood she started flashing her tits. I was in heaven!

The Scorpions loved it as well; they started giving me the thumbs up which stunned me. The main act loved me as much as I loved them. Yeah, my new girlfriend was flashing her tits at them, but I didn't care, the Scorpions were paying attention to me! Plus, Stacey was feeling me up and my dick was hard as a rock. This was true rock 'n' roll and it was fucking awesome!

As the night ended, things got better. The band's big security guy came up to us.

"Hey, the Scorpions want to meet you guys," he said.

"You mean backstage?" I asked.

"Hell, yes!"

"Really, no way!"

"Yep, it's your lucky night. Follow me."

We weaved through security and got to the final gate. I was still in a state of shock. I was having one of the best nights of my life. My mind was racing. *I can't believe that in a few seconds I'll be backstage with the Scorpions!*

Stacey walked through the gate and I followed. The big security guy stepped in front of me.

"Hey, I'm with her," I said. *Did he suddenly forget that?*

"No, you're not!" He said. I looked up at him dumbfounded and he stared back with a blank expression.

"What? Yes, I am! We were *together* in the front row. You told us to come back *together*. We're supposed to go backstage and meet the band!"

"Nope, just her."

"Yeah, but she's with me."

"Not anymore."

I started to panic. My perfect night was suddenly falling apart.

"Hey, Stacey! STACEY! They won't let me back! WAIT UP!"

Stacey never turned around, leaving me in the dust. I watched her walk down the hall and disappear. I was crushed!

FUCK YOU, SCORPIONS!

I was mad at the Scorpions for a year after that. I threw out all their albums. If anybody said their name, I would curse them out. I hated the fucking Scorpions.

Of course, looking back, I see what was going on. I had a bad mustache and a mullet. I looked like a dirty Mexican. Why would they want me backstage? I would've asked them dumb questions like how did you come up with the artwork for your last album? Who gives a fuck? Plus, on a scale of one to ten, I was a four. This chick was a nine. She used me to get up front. She let me squeeze her tits a few times and then got to party with the Scorpions. I drove home with blue balls and a soggy six in my underwear leaking clear stuff.

SUPER BOWL BULLSHIT

Enough of these awful pop acts that get booked for the halftime show. Every year it's the same show.

There will be eighty backup dancers doing the same stupid fucking moves that Madonna and her dancers did in 1982.

Wow! How fucking original! They need that many people on-stage to distract you from their lack of talent. I'm a comic. Imagine if I had dancers onstage with me jumping around after I told the punchline? An audience member would turn to their friend and say, "What was the punchline?"

He'd say, "I have no idea I was watching those three guys behind him do backflips."

There is one thing you can count on when you have these awful pop acts doing the halftime show—they won't have to do a sound check. Why? Because the microphones will be *turned off* during the performance!

Seriously, who among all the people that watch the NFL every Sunday is a Katy Perry or a Beyoncé fan?

NOBODY!

Not even the fantasy football nerds care about this bullshit. You know who likes that garbage? Sixteen-year-old girls! That's who will watch a Lady Gaga Super Bowl halftime show.

I know the dumb logic behind the NFL. They think, *we know that guys will watch. So, let's get the women to watch as well!* But, even if you get sixteen-year-old girls to watch that twelve-minute segment, it doesn't mean you've made them fans of the Super Bowl or the NFL as a whole. As soon as the show is over, they'll go back into their bedrooms and stare at their phones like they do twenty-four hours a day. They won't watch the third and fourth quarter because they loved the halftime show! They won't tune into the Pro Bowl or the NFL Draft in April.

I remember a few years ago when Beyoncé did the halftime show and the decision backfired on the NFL. Women that like the "Single Ladies" song hovered around the TV set to watch. Beyoncé had just had a baby six weeks before and she came onstage looking amazing but then all the women watching got jealous.

"Yeah, well if I had the money for seven personal trainers I could look like that, too," one woman said.

"Wouldn't it be great if I could afford a personal chef to cook me healthy meals," another woman said.

Then, even before the show was over, the women went back to the kitchen, one by one, to drown their sorrows and drink more wine and feel even worse about themselves.

Do you want an interesting halftime show for real NFL fans? Put Adrian Peterson and Ray Rice in a steel cage match. The rules should be that Ray Rice can only use his left hook and Adrian Peterson uses a tree branch.

I'll watch that—EVERY FUCKING MINUTE!

Part Two: Awful Conversations

Why are people so fucking stupid? Why do people have to fuck up normal, everyday communication? The amount of awful conversations I endure on a weekly basis is overwhelming. Simple trips to a grocery store or restaurant leave me drowning in some horrific dialogue. A flood of shitty slang words, dipshit definitions, and horrible abbreviations assaults me no matter where I go.

Most of these awful words start in places like the rap music community. White people think hip-hop slang is cool so they use it to avoid seeming corny. But, it has the opposite effect because these words are often worse than the original expressions.

If you are a young kid, I get it. Kids want to fit in. Kids want to know what the new taboo words mean. If you are kid at a party and everybody else is using a new slang word, you use the word, because you want to get laid. You want to have friends. You want to connect with people. I have no problem with that.

My problem is with the adults who use these awful words because they want sound cool. I have to listen to a thirty-year-old soccer mom say something like, "I'm having din-din at the famjam with my bae!"

If you are like me, you want to avoid people like this at all costs. That's why I'm using Part Two of *Everybody Is Awful* to shine the spotlight on *Awful Conversations*.

Slang Words That Suck!

Throwing Shade
Verb [throh-ing sheyd]
Slang for: Disrespecting someone or making fun of someone

Anyone that uses *throwing shade* deserves disrespect. I can't imagine using this phrase in front of my friend and fellow comedian, Jim Norton.

Let's say I called him up and said, "Hey Norton, I was onstage last night doing comedy and a heckler started *throwing shade* at me."

The next thing I would hear would be a *click* as Jim hung up on me. Then, I would get a text from him saying, "The call didn't drop! I heard what you said and it was fucking awful. It's been good knowing you!"

He'd forgive me for fucking his girlfriend long before he'd forgive me for using that phrase. In fact, it wouldn't surprise me if he skipped my funeral because I said something like *throwing shade*.

Our twenty-five-year-old friendship would be over and I wouldn't blame him. That's what I get for trying to sound like a cool teenager when I'm a middle-aged man.

Baby
Noun [bey-bee]
Slang for: One's favorite possessions

Some douche bought a used Corvette and referred to it as his *baby*.

You realize your car was bought at a used car dealership. It was traded in last week. It was fucking disgusting when it came in. The previous owner was a fat slob who sat in your *baby*, picked his nose, and flicked his boogers on the dash.

He farted in that seat you currently sit in and even shit himself a time or two while he was stuck in traffic. I'm sure he had sex with his chick in there and blew a load all over the seats when he did it. His sweaty ass crack was rubbing a stain in the driver's seat while he was fucking her. But you wouldn't know that because they cleaned it up, detailed the thing, sprayed some Ozium air sanitizer in there, and then scammed you into buying it. So, have fun with your *baby*!

Hundy
Noun [huhn-dee]
Slang for: One hundred dollars

When I first heard the word *hundy*, I thought someone was talking about that shitty Korean car—the Hyundai. It's much worse than that!

Douchebags that play Texas Hold 'Em use the word *hundy* when they're betting. I guess it makes them feel like losing hundreds of dollars is no big deal. To me it sounds like hipster-wannabe, asshole talk.

I hated the fucking hipster poker players already. Those dicks wear sunglasses and fucking hoodies because they don't want you to read their face when they fucking bet. They look like assholes. Now, when they say *hundy* they sound like assholes. Where is George Zimmerman when you need him?

I hope when these hipster gamblers are betting a *hundy* with their hoodie and sunglasses, their wife is at home sucking off the neighbor. I bet she wears a hoodie and sunglasses when she leaves his house so the other neighbors don't know what's going on. Also, I hope she spends a *hundy* of your gambling money to dry-clean cum stains out of her dress.

Vajayjay
Noun [vuh-jey-jey]
Slang for: Vagina

Oprah was the one who brought this word out into the mainstream. She asked on her show, "Is *vajayjay* a good word because vagina sounds dirty?" So all the fucking goofy soccer moms who watch Oprah started using *vajayjay*.

Women need to stop calling their snatch a *vajayjay* unless they're trying to make sure men will never touch it, eat it, or fuck it. If a hot chick came up to me and said, "Would you like to see my *vajayjay*?" I'd tell her I'd rather see my Mom get carjacked.

Ressies
Noun [rez-eez]
Slang for: Reservations made at a restaurant

The first time I heard this I was on a date with a girl. We were waiting at the hostess station and the woman in front of me said, "We would like a table for two but we didn't make any *ressies*."

The hostesses said, "That's okay, it's a slow night. You don't need *ressies* to get a table."

When my date told me what that word meant I told her I wanted to leave immediately. I'd rather eat at Taco Bell than a place that uses this slang word. Sure, I'll be shitting for the next three days and my ass will be on fire from eating their garbage food. But, at least I don't have to make *ressies* to eat there and it won't cost me a *hundy*. Their tacos taste better than a *vajayjay* anyway!

Chillaxing
Verb [chill-lax-ing]
Slang for: When you're chilling so much that you are relaxing
Horrendous!

If you're chilling you're pretty much relaxing already. How can you be doing both? How much fucking relaxing are you doing? Are you meditating or something like that? Or, are you just sitting on a couch watching a game? Because then you'd just be chilling. You don't have to throw relaxing in there too, we get it, you're lazy! You're probably unemployed, too. You've got no friends and nobody wants to be near you. You're fucking lonely and have no job skills and you're just milking the fucking government, collecting unemployment. Why don't you do everyone a favor and go chillax in a coffin!

Dipshit Definitions

Man Crush
Noun [man krush]
Definition: A non-sexual relationship between two men

Everyone knows what a crush means. When you had a crush on someone in high school that meant you wanted to go out with him or her and hopefully it would lead to sex. If the other person just wanted to be friends with you it drove you nuts. So whenever I hear a guy say he has a man crush on another guy, I take it to mean that he wants to suck his dick if he could.

Chicks are always saying that their man has a man crush on Tom Brady. No, he doesn't. The reason he spends a lot of time talking about him and looking at highlights of him on ESPN is because he doesn't want to talk to you.

Mongo

Adjective [mahn-goh]

Definition: Used to describe something extremely large or important

Mongo is another awful word that people use to emphasize being a huge fan of a sports team. We get it that you like your team, asshole. You don't need to ruin things with the word *mongo*! You're a *mongo* fan because sports distract you from dealing with the deeper issues in your life. Just because you know everything about the Jets doesn't make you a *mongo* Jets fan.

Mongo fans think they are *mongo* fans because they wear team jerseys. Wearing your jersey to the sports bar just means you're a child. The only time it's acceptable to wear a team jersey is if you're with your kid and you both have them on. Other than that, a grown person with their name on the back of a jersey is a fucking douche. Not one person finds that amusing or cool. Everyone is thinking the same thing, *What an ass! Why would you leave the house with that on?*

Next time I see a jersey-wearing dick I'll ask him, "Shouldn't you be on the sidelines with the team? What are you doing here? Your team already has five guys out for injuries. I'm sure they could use a *mongo* motherfucker like you who weighs one hundred and twenty pounds, wears nerd glasses, and has six beers in him, right!

This is why I really hope my son is not into sports. If I heard him say, "I'm a *mongo* fan." I'll take him out of my will.

Foodie

Noun [foo-dee]

Definition: A person who knows a lot about food and posts pictures of their dinner on Facebook and captions it "food porn"

If it's *food porn* I should want to fuck it when I look at it. But, I look at these photos and I never get a hard on. I just look at it and think, *here's another person bragging about what they're going to eat.*

You're just a douchebag who likes food. You're not a foodie; you're probably a FATTIE! Too bad you can't be a GYMIE and go to the fucking gym!

Famjam

Noun [fam-jam]

Definition: A party that consists of only family members

A jam is when musicians get together and play music, but a family at a *famjam* is not jamming on anything but misery. It's a miracle if a family get-together is fun. Usually, family members are bitter and jealous of each other. They spend the whole time trying to impress each other with the materialistic shit they own.

There are unresolved issues from childhood that surface when families get together. One family member thinks he didn't get enough attention growing up. Another one is still resentful over something that happened when he was five years old. Most of the time getting together with family is nothing but drama.

There is a reason most families live in different parts of the United States. They don't like to spend time with each other. Don't call this a *famjam*, call it what it really is—a get-together with a bunch of whiny cunts!

Threenager

Noun [three-ney-jer]

Definition: A three-year-old possessing the attitude of a teenager

There is something disgusting about pretending your child is older than his actual age. Your toddler isn't a teen or a fucking *threenager*. He's just like every other little kid. If he doesn't have fucking pubes, he's not a *threenager*. If he's not jerking off like a maniac, he's not a *threenager*. That's what teenage boys do.

Is your hand cream missing? Is he taking two-hour showers because he's whacking his bag? Are there smudges all over your iPad screen from his lubed up fingers touching it? No? You know why? Because he's not a *threenager*; he's a fucking three-year-old! Now go check his diaper to see if he has a load of shit in it.

Kiddos
Noun [kid-dohz]
Definition: Nickname that parents call their kids

You will hear some mom say, "Just put the kiddos to bed." That woman is not fun. She's never said, "Honey, I just put the kiddos to bed. Let's fuck."

Any woman who says *kiddos* doesn't really like fucking. She will sit there or lie there because her husband finally painted the garage. Other than that, she's a complete dud in the sack.

When they do have sex, her kids are on her mind the whole time. In the middle of it she will say, "I hope the kiddos don't hear us." There's a real good thing to say in the middle of having sex. How would they hear anything when there is not a peep coming out of her mouth? The only thing they might hear is the guy yelling, "I just lost my fucking hard-on!"

Babymoon
Noun [bey-bee-moon]
Definition: A vacation like a honeymoon planned before the birth of a child

Any expectant parent that plans a *babymoon* should consider adoption. Fuck, that word makes me cringe! Just say, "We're going away for a few days because when the baby comes it'll be crazy."

Is a *babymoon* fun for a woman? She's seven months pregnant. She's fat and her back hurts. She has cankles. She feels like shit, looks like shit, needs to take a shit, but can't on the plane because she doesn't fit in the fucking bathroom.

Her hemorrhoids have flared up. Her roots have grown out. She can't use hair dye. She can't drink. She can't smoke. She doesn't want to fuck her husband. Her husband doesn't want to fuck her. Wow! Sounds like this *babymoon* will be the best trip of their lives!

When she gets there it's too hot for her to hang at the pool. She can't Jet Ski, hike, or zip line. Basically, she flew to another country to sit in a hotel room. If she does feel like having sex with her husband he'll use the excuse that he's afraid his penis will hit the baby. Meanwhile, he's a white Irish guy. Even his wife were crowning at the time he still wouldn't hit the baby in the head. But, he shouldn't worry. It's a *babymoon*! He should celebrate and fuck his fat wife!

Abbreviations for Assholes

Delish
Adjective [duh-lish]
Abbreviation for: Delicious

If Scarlett Johansson came up to me, pulled her pants down, put her snatch right in my face, and said, "Here, taste it, it's *delish*!" I would get up and walk away just because she used that word.

Froyo
Noun [froh-yoh]
Abbreviation for: Frozen yogurt

Who the fuck says, "You want to get some *froyo*?"

If you said that to me, I'd fro you off a fucking cliff. When the police question me about your mangled body, I'll tell them the fucking truth. "I pushed him because he's a grown man and he asked me if I wanted to get some *froyo*."

I know the police wouldn't fuck with me. They'd say, "I understand why you did it, you're free to go!"

My worst nightmare is riding home from dinner with new friends and someone asks, "Hey, you want to stop and get some *froyo* before we go home?" The moment I heard *froyo*, I would open the car door and do a tuck-and-roll into oncoming traffic.

Bloody
Noun [bluh-dee]
Abbreviation for: A Bloody Mary cocktail

Don Jamieson and I were in this restaurant having lunch and he ordered a Bloody Mary. Thirty minutes later, the waiter notices he's finished and asks, "You want another *bloody*?" I threw up in my mouth!

Ask a table of chicks if they want a *bloody*, not two guys wearing Black Sabbath T-shirts. Know your customers if you're a waiter. Why would any guy ask another guy if they want a *bloody*? Anyone who uses that abbreviation should get his mouth bloodied!

Deets
Plural Noun [deets]
Abbreviation for: Details

Shortening the word details to *deets* is reprehensible. *Deets* is five letters. *Details* is seven. You're saving two letters by saying *deets*.

If someone asked, "Can you give me the *deets* for the *froyo* place?"

I'd say, "Sure, pull out of your driveway and make a left into a fucking tree!"

Brolly
Noun [brah-lee]
Abbreviation for: Umbrella

Brolly doesn't even make fucking sense as an abbreviation. *Brella* would make more sense even though it's just as fucking horrendous. What the fuck is a *brolly*?

If someone had a gun to my head and said, "Either you say the word *brolly* or I open this umbrella up in your ass!" I would bend over and pull my ass cheeks apart.

Natty Ice
Proper Noun [nat-ee ayss]
Abbreviation for: The brand of beer called Natural Ice

The only term for Natural Ice beer people should use is *SHIT*! Because that's what it is!

Natty Ice must be a generational thing. When I was growing up the shit beer was Old Milwaukee. We didn't call it *Old Mil*, though. We said the whole fucking name just like it was meant to be said as you should.

Shit beer can serve a purpose. When I was younger, we would bring a case of Old Milwaukee to a house party and nobody would want to drink it. Then, we would drink everyone else's beer until it was gone and have the case of Old Milwaukee to ourselves. Perfect!

Dunkies
Proper noun [duhn-kees]
Abbreviation for: Dunkin' Donuts

Hearing about the abbreviation *dunkies* made me want Dunkin' Donuts to go out of business. How is Dunkin' Donuts still in business anyway? It's truly awful. When are people going to realize that they're adults now, and they shouldn't be eating donuts. I'd rather have the Ebola virus.

I believe the assholes that love their shit coffee came up with the abbreviation *Dunkies*. If someone asked me if I wanted anything at *Dunkies,* I'd tell them to pick up a coffin. Why? Because when you get back home, I'm going to snap your fucking neck.

Bae
Noun [bey]
Abbreviation for: Before Anyone Else

The first time I saw the word *Bae* was on Facebook. A chick posted, "*Bae* won't watch the movie *Sweet Home Alabama* with me!" If you use this revolting nickname for your significant other, keep it to yourself. It's a fucking horrible abbreviation!

Bae won't watch *Sweet Home Alabama* because you call him *Bae* and because he has a cock in his pants. The movie he wants to watch is *Sweet Home Ass Bangers,* a porn movie he has downloaded on the basement computer. If you're his true *Bae,* let him go jerk off to that while you watch your stupid romantic comedy.

Za
Noun [zah]
Abbreviation for: Pizza and Zombie Apocalypse

Are people so lazy that they can't even say the word *pizza*? You have to say *'za*? I would die of starvation before I would use that word.

People also use ZA for Zombie Apocalypse. Let's stop with that shit. There will never be a zombie apocalypse! Stop smoking weed and watching goofy TV shows about zombies.

Is there a history of zombie attacks I don't know about? Hold on. Let me go look it up. Okay, I just searched Google and it said: *No asshole, zombies are make believe!*

Fuck your ZA, nerd! Go to Comic-Con and die!

Brekkie
Noun [breh-kee]
Abbreviation for: An Australian breakfast

Australia, please tell me you don't use *brekkie* to describe breakfast. I've never been to your country but I love everything I've learned about it. I really want to visit because it seems like Australian people are rough around the edges and not so politically correct. The guys play rugby, go to the bar to get hammered, and get into fights. That's fucking beautiful!

I can't imagine a tough, macho, Australian dude using the word *brekkie*. But, maybe it happens? Is it common? Do men respond to waitresses by saying, "I'm not going to order anything right now, I had a big *brekkie* this morning!"

Please tell me if that happens, every dude at the table will take their heavy fucking beer mugs and smash them in that guy's face! How about that for a fucking *brekkie*?

Donzies

Adjective [duhn-zees]

Abbreviation for: Being done

Donzies is so bad I think it's the reason Ray Rice hit his fiancée in the elevator. They were hanging in a casino and Ray Rice probably said he wanted to play one more round of blackjack. She argued and said, "Not me, I'm *donzies*!" What happened after that is on the security footage.

That's why the commissioner of the NFL only suspended Rice for two games. He intended to suspend him for the entire season but then he heard Ray's girlfriend used the word *donzies*. That changed everything!

I think he said, "Ray, I don't condone what you did but I don't blame you either."

This chapter is DONZIES!

CHAPTER NINE

SNUFF CALLS

The success of *Crank Yankers* took my career to another level. During breaks from the show Don Jamieson and I recorded calls for a new *Terrorizing Telemarketers* comedy album. This is when our creative process hit a new level of insanity. So, we pushed the envelope with each new prank call, making up crazier premises every time we recorded. We had no idea that this new material would get us into serious trouble.

It finally happened on a night when I was recording alone. I remember the exact moment, it was eight o'clock on a weeknight, prime time for telemarketers, and I got an interesting call.

"Mr. Florentine, this is your new credit card company calling with a *great* deal. Today we are offering an *immediate* transfer of five thousand dollars! We will move this money from your credit line to your personal bank account at no charge to you."

"Okay," I say. "What's the catch?"

"There's no catch. All we need is your bank account information and we can process this as a wire transfer—immediately!"

"Five thousand dollars? That's a lot of money!"

"Well, we know things come up, and many of our customers need emergency funds. We want to help and make sure you're prepared for any unexpected circumstance. That's why we called."

When the telemarketer mentioned an *emergency,* the wheels in my head spun—a seriously demented idea formed in my mind.

"Oh, that's great you want to help. I do have an emergency! You see, I just hit this old lady with my car yesterday. Now they are telling me I'll have to pay all of her medical bills!"

I hear nothing but dead silence on the other end of the line. That told me I'd hit a nerve. The hook was set. I start expanding my story to reel her in.

"I just came back from visiting the old woman at the hospital," I tell the telemarketer. "When I was there I noticed that I knocked out all of her teeth. I should start with that. Do you know how much a new set of choppers cost?"

I could tell there was a tiny part of the telemarketer that wanted to hang up. However, this con artist was so desperate to make the money transfer, and get her bonus, she ignored her common sense.

"Well sir, I think new teeth would cost somewhere around three hundred dollars, but I'm not positive."

I had raised the stakes and she didn't flinch. I kept going.

"How about a new walker? I demolished the one she had. I crushed it under my car."

"Maybe four hundred dollars?" She says.

"Oh man, okay. So, I heard she's going to have to wear diapers from here on out. What's a year's supply of those going to run me?"

"That has to be a hundred dollars a month. For twelve months, you are looking at twelve to fifteen hundred dollars. This is adding up, sir. It looks like you're definitely going to need the five thousand dollar advance. What's your bank account information, I'll transfer it right now!"

Obviously, I'm not interested in this deal, but I go for her jugular and blurt out something without thinking about the possible repercussions.

"You know what, I don't want to waste all that money on this old bag! I'll just go down to the hospital and kill that old lady!"

Silence.

At this point, she finally gives in.

"I'm hanging up, sir," she says.

"Look, I'm going to the hospital right now and smother the old bitch with a pillow. I'll be back home soon. Call me in about an hour and we can work this transfer out. Thanks for your help!"

Click!

Click! Here Come the Cops!

Twenty minutes later, the fun was over. I had a surprise at my door— two very serious-looking New Jersey detectives were on my porch.

"Are you Mr. James Florentine?" One scowling cop asked me.

The call had backfired. The telemarketer called the police in my town because she had all my information right in front of her.

"Yeah, I'm Jim Florentine," I said in my friendliest voice.

"Can we come in?"

"Yeah, what's this about?"

"You were just on a phone call where you said you were going to go kill an old lady?"

Oh, shit! I start pleading my case.

"Yeah, I said that, but I was messing around. I do these prank calls and I was just trying to get her off the phone."

"Let me see your identification," one detective demanded.

While I pulled out my driver's license, I noticed the other cop walking through the house. He was poking his head in every room.

"Can I ask what you're doing, officer?"

"I'm looking for the victim—a *corpse!*"

Holy shit! Now I start to panic!

"Look, I work on this prank call show called *Crank Yankers*. It's a television show on Comedy Central. I don't know if you've ever watched it? I'm the guy that goes, *Yaay, I got mail, I got mail!* and *Bread makes me poop!* Have you seen the show?"

The two detectives just stare at me like I'm a total idiot.

One of them notices the recorder hooked up to the phone and ask me what I'm doing with it.

"I sit by the phone all day and wait for telemarketers to call so I can pull pranks on them. I record the calls and I put them out on CDs."

He checks my driver's license again.

"You're thirty-four years old. What the fuck is wrong with you?" He throws my license at me. "We don't have a problem with you doing prank calls but don't threaten anyone," he says.

"Of course, no problem."

"You should know something, if we find a dead old lady in this area we're coming back for you. You'll be our number-one suspect! You got that?"

What the fuck? A suspect? I was in shock things had turned on me so fast.

"Don't worry you guys will *never* hear from me again—I promise!"

The cops leave and I finally get it through my thick head, there are limits to these prank calls. I promise myself I'll be more careful next time.

Guess what, it takes a lot for me to learn my lesson. That was not the last time prank calls landed me in trouble. Two weeks after the old lady call, I was facing six months in jail for another prank call gone wrong. Keep reading and you will see what a piece of garbage I am.

Awful Shopping: Bagging the Grocery Store

The infamous *Old Lady Snuff Call* taught me many things. One of the biggest lessons was learning that some salespeople and businesses will do just about anything to make a buck. Unfortunately, for all the normal people in the world, those high-pressure sales tactics have migrated over to other businesses. You can't buy a fucking pack of gum without someone up-selling you. That's one reason shopping has become so awful. You can't walk into a store without being hassled by the staff, like you're getting cross-examined on the witness stand.

What the Fuck Are You Doing Here?

One of the worst places to shop is the fucking grocery store!

When I go to the supermarket I'm determined to get what I need and get the fuck out—as fast as possible! Like most people, I usually have a long list of things to do and want to get back to my work or life. People who take their time in a supermarket must not be happy at home. They hate their spouse so they kill time wandering aimlessly down aisles filled with things they are never going to buy. And if these dummies see you ducking in to get milk, they stop you and chat you up. I hate having conversations in the middle of the grocery store. Meet me at the bar down the street and we'll have a beer, but don't make small talk about the weather. I know it's hot out. That's why I have shorts on jerk-off!

There is one question I despise more than any other: *Hey, what are you doing here?*

I insist on answering them like this:

"What are you doing here?" they ask.

"I'm here to buy a new sports car. What are you doing here?" I say.

"A car? Come on *really*, what are you doing here?"

"I'm actually here to get my dog circumcised. They have a special promotion in the pet food aisle. What are you doing here?"

"I'm food shopping."

"Oh, they have *food* here?"

"Of course they do! Seriously, what are you doing here?"

"You're probably not going to believe this but my son and I get hungry from time to time and we run out of food so we come here. Anything else fuck face?"

Cart Creeps

Normal people keep their carts up against the shelf so other shoppers can get around them with no problem. That's just proper shopping cart etiquette. But then you always have those self-entitled cunts that block the aisle without a care in the world.

Most of the time, the best thing is to say excuse me and just push their cart over a bit and cruise on by. Then, you get the assholes that give you attitude. They narrow their eyes at you as if to say, "Oh, *sorrrrry*! Was I in your way?"

That infuriates me.

"Yeah, you are in my way! Your fucking cart is in the way and your fucking damn kid is in my way. The world doesn't revolve around you, jerk-off!"

Sometimes, when I see someone walking away from their cart and it's blocking the aisle I approach them like they are a store employee.

"Hey, just wanted you to know, some rude and obnoxious person who doesn't give a shit about anyone else, just left that cart in the middle of the aisle. Maybe you should take the cart up to customer service because it looks like they've abandoned it."

"Sorry, that's my cart," they usually say.

The response on their face is beautiful. The next time I roll by that ass the aisle is clear enough to land a 747!

On Thin Slice

Awful grocery shoppers always walk around the store with an entitled attitude. The one thing I don't understand is why they hassle the deli workers. Who decided it was okay to tell the deli guy how to do his job?

How many times have you heard someone say this?

"Give me half a pound of turkey breast but don't cut it too thick. Slice it really thin!"

What the fuck? Now this poor stiff behind the counter has to slice a piece and show it to you to see if it meets your approval. Then he's going to get his balls busted because you think the meat is sliced too thick.

What in the hell is the difference if it's thick or thin?

You're just making a fucking sandwich at home. The meat is going between two slices of thick bread with tomatoes, onions, lettuce, and mustard.

If he cuts it thick just count that as one slice on your sandwich. If he cuts it thin, you count it as two. It's the same fucking weight. It's the same amount of turkey!

Then these assholes want to taste the product.

They ask for a pound of Provolone cheese but demand a slice to check the taste. Then, everyone has to stand there and watch him or her stuff their face.

It is Provolone cheese. It tastes like *fucking* Provolone cheese!

Thick or thin, I hope you choke on it!

Rotten Crotch Fruit

Then you have those people that drag their hungry, tired, and out-of-control children into the grocery store. Bringing little kids in the supermarket is usually a problem. You have to do it in the right way. If I take my young son shopping, I make sure he is well rested. Don't take a tired kid to the store. Wait until he gets up from his nap. You don't have to get your shopping done now. People at your house aren't dying from starvation.

I've also noticed parents who take a cranky kid with them are always yelling!

"Put that back! Put that back! I *said* put it back!"

I just want to say, "Hey asshole, your kid is three. He doesn't understand the concept of putting it back. *You put it back! You brought him here. You put him in this situation! Don't fucking yell at him. It's your fault, not his!*"

Are you trying to show off? Are you trying to prove that you're a great parent by disciplining your kid in front of everyone? No one is applauding you for that. No one thinks you're a great parent. They think you're an *asshole* for taking an exhausted kid to the store.

If the kid grabs a bag of chips just take it away, and say in a real low voice, "No, no, you can't have that." Then, just put it back.

Don't you know bringing your dumb kid down the fucking candy or snack aisle is a bad move? He will want everything he sees. He'll grab at everything, scream, and cry because he can't have it.

An awful parent always says, "Yeah, he should know better. I need to teach him he can't have candy all the time."

No, he doesn't know better, asshole! Now everyone in the store has to listen to the two of you scream at each other. It's your fault because you're the one who raised him on candy, anyway. You're the one who gave it to him when he did something good and now you brought him down the fucking candy and snack aisle.

That's like picking up your friend at rehab and taking him to a party where everyone is snorting coke off a stripper's ass.

DUNKIN' DONUTS STINKS!

I'm not a fan of Dunkin' Donuts.

Their coffee tastes burnt. Their donuts taste stale.

The worst part is their sales techniques. They ask you the most ridiculous questions when you go up to the register.

I only go to a Dunkin' Donuts out of sheer desperation, usually when I can't find a Starbucks. Every time I'm in that store, it's the same bullshit:

"Hello what can I get for you today?"

"Let me have a regular coffee to go. Make it a large. Thanks."

"Do you want any donuts with that?"

"No sir, I don't. I'm not a child anymore that likes donuts. That's so weird you ask that question. I didn't know you sold donuts here. I mean I know the place is called *Dunkin' Donuts* and I see that there are one million donuts on a rack behind you. Are you telling me I can *buy* them here? You are throwing me for a fucking loop!"

Enough with this shit, *all right*!

Half the Dunkin' Donuts are connected to gas stations. The rule of thumb is that you will not get a good cup of coffee inside an Exxon station. Nobody working in a gas station gives a fuck about making good coffee.

Also, I'm sick of their shitty catchphrases. None of these retarded slogans catch on. For instance, they've beat us over the head with:

"America runs on Dunkin'!"

No it doesn't! If all the Dunkin' Donuts closed tomorrow, America would still be up and running. We don't need donuts to save America!

They've even tried to be hip by abbreviating Dunkin' Donuts.

"Hey America, start your day at D. D."

Nobody is calling Dunkin' Donuts "D. D."

Stop wasting money on these ad campaigns and concentrate on making fresher coffee and fresher donuts. How about doing that?

Now the new marketing campaign is targeting social media. They tell customers, "Go to Dunkin' Donuts and take a picture. Then put it on Twitter or Instagram with the hashtag #DunkinMoment."

Beyond brutal.
You know what my #DunkinMoment is?
I had some of your nasty coffee, it went right through me, and
I went into the bathroom and dropped a D. D.—a double deuce!
That's my #DunkinMoment! Dunkin' Donuts stinks!!

Awful Shopping: Checkout Hell

One thing that makes shopping so awful is the checkout line, especially when you have someone awful in front of you.

Divide & Conquer

The checkout divider freaks people out. I'll refuse to use it just to mess with someone in front of me. It drives people crazy.

I'll intentionally put my items an inch away from their mound of groceries. They can't stand that our purchases may be mixed up.

One time, this fat guy kept looking back and whipping me dirty looks. He was waiting for me to put the divider down. I finally had to say something:

"Sir, you weigh 450 pounds and you are buying Doritos, Ben & Jerry's, Cheetos, Twinkies, and M&Ms. Anyone looking at that pile of junk food knows those are your items. My grilled chicken and fresh fruit is just an inch behind your pile of shit. *Nobody* will confuse our orders. Our cashier will look at you, then look at the food, and immediately figure it out—the fresh fruit is not for the *fat fuck*!"

In the Fucking Bag!

For some reason when I'm buying a gallon of water, the cashier won't put it in a bag. Sure, the water jug has a handle on it but it's a lot easier to carry it in a bag.

They put the gallon of milk in a bag but not the water. Why? I don't fucking get it. The cashier scans my water and asks:

"You want this in a bag?"

"Yeah, just like everything else," I say.

Most of the time, they don't offer you a bag for the water. If I ask for a bag, they look at me like I'm an asshole. *What the fuck?*

Sometimes I can't help myself, and I say, "You put three gallons of milk in bags for me, why not the water?"

One cashier actually said, "Well . . . it's *water!*"

What the fuck does that mean? I know it's water. That's the reason I bought it. I needed water. Thanks for reminding me that this clear stuff in a gallon jug labeled water—is *water*. I thought I was buying a gallon of vodka. Too bad your father didn't wear a *bag* that night you were conceived!

Line-Cutting Cunts

One of the worst things awful shoppers do is cut the checkout line. Don't think for one minute you are getting in front of me because you have a few things and I have a full cart! Back the fuck off, motherfucker!

You have three items, and you get behind me when I have thirty. Now, I have to feel pressure to let you ahead of me.

That's exactly what always happens with these assholes. They stand behind you juggling their two or three items. They tap their foot impatiently. Huff and puff because it's taking a long time. Or, they have the balls to ask if they can cut the line.

"It's not my fault you aren't in the express line, you fuck!"

I have a solution. I've invented a checklist that screens out awful shopping habits. If someone wants to cut the line and can pass the checklist then I'm happy to let them go ahead of me.

The Awful Shopper's Guide to Cutting the Line

❏ **Are you paying by check?**

We live in a time when nobody should ever pay by check at the grocery store. If you insist on being an asshole and using a check, at least do a little prep work before you get to the store. You know the name of the supermarket, so fill that in before you get in line. Also, fill in the date, the signature, and even the memo section. That way when the cashier gives you the total, you can write the amount and you're done. That's a pretty fucking simple, and idiot-proof, way to handle paying by check!

Don't ask, "Who should I make this check out to?" Let's see, you're in a *Kroger* store, why don't you make it out to *Whole Foods*!

❏ **Are you paying with loose change?**

Are you paying with loose change? Well, don't do that unless you're prepared.

Have it in your hand ready to go. Don't wait until the cashier says, "Ok, that will be $154.46" to dig through your purse looking for that precious forty-six cents.

How about doing a little prep work here too? Have ninety-nine cents in your hand as you approach the register. Whatever the change amount is, just subtract from the ninety-nine cents. Pretty simple, huh? Why is this so easy for me and I only graduated from community college?

❏ **Do you have coupons?**

I've had enough with people using coupons at the supermarket. I wish every store had a specific coupon register called the *I'm-a-Cheap-Fuck Aisle* so all of us noncheap fucks won't have to wait while these tightwads work their scheme to save twenty cents. Half the time they forget to give the cashier the right coupon at the right time and hold up the line while they make sure their total is adjusted.

Of course, there is always some kind of discrepancy. Then, they get mad and start digging through all the bagged groceries. Finally, they find they have the wrong brand of yogurt and a coupon catastrophe begins—they can't use their worthless ten-cent rebate!

"Oh no! I thought my coupon was for Dannon. Now I have to pay full price for the other brand!" They bellow.

Yeah, you have to pay the full price, asshole! It costs ten fucking pennies more. You drove here in a Range Rover. You are wearing an expensive watch. I don't think a *dime* will hurt your bottom line. So, dig into your $5,000 Louis Vuitton purse for an extra dime and move the fuck on!

❏ Will you be requesting a price check?

Only a cheap fuck would request a price check over a small price discrepancy. Everyone knows a price check forces the cashier to call the store manager who then calls a stock boy who then identifies the price and finally runs up to the front with the information. Meanwhile, there is a line of grumpy people waiting, getting more and more pissed off by the second.

They don't hear the kids melting down and grabbing the impulse items and throwing them all over the floor. They don't have a clue every single person behind them is making plans to run them over in the parking lot.

❏ Will you stop the cashier for a halftime subtotal?

Don't ask the cashier to check the total in the middle of ringing you up. If you only have a certain amount of money, you should track that while you shop. Don't put the responsibility on other people.

While you shop, use a fucking calculator on your phone. Add the shit up as you put it in the cart! The only time you should make the cashier stop in the middle of ringing you up is if your wife all of a sudden hits menopause in line and you need to go put the tampons back.

❑ **Will you be leaving the register because you forgot something?**

Stop going to the supermarket with no plan. Make a list. Put it on your phone. Put it on a piece of paper. Know what you're doing when you get in there.

As soon as I walk in, I'm focused. I go to produce first, then the deli, and then over to dairy. Next, I hit the meat counter, then the paper aisle, and then I'm out. Making a plan like that is simple. It's similar to the plan I have when I have a one-night stand. I make sure it's consensual, I "usually" wear a condom, and then afterwards I give her the wrong phone number.

❑ **When the product doesn't scan are you going to crack a corny joke?**

Sometimes items don't scan properly. When that happens there is always some jerk who cracks the joke, "Well, I guess it's free then!"

I know telling a joke doesn't hold up the line, but that joke stinks!

Don't you realize the cashier hears that cornball shit fifty times a day? It's never funny and you will never get free groceries because the scanner didn't work. So don't fucking repeat that joke ever again!

Whenever people tell this joke, they'll turn and look back at whoever is behind them, wanting to get a laugh. When that happens, I stare back at them like I want to stab them in the fucking chest with the checkout divider!

For Faster Service . . . Fart!

The only experience I really *enjoy* in a supermarket is the smell of someone's farts.

I know it bothers many people but I can't say anything bad about it because farts are always funny. I don't mind walking into a fart. When I do, I can't help cracking the fuck up.

Going to the grocery store with my father was probably the only time in my life that I liked the fucking place. My dad had the funniest time-saving tactic I've ever seen. He also had the balls to use it repeatedly, which made trips to store great.

I guess my impatience with shopping had its origin with Dad. He hated waiting so much he was willing to do something drastic about it. For instance, if there were a long line at the deli counter, he would go right up to the front of the line, hover near the people waiting, and cut a nasty gasser!

Within seconds, his nasty crowd splitter did its work. Everybody would clear out of the way. My father looked like Moses parting the Red Sea. While his victims were coughing and gagging, he'd walk through the crowd right up to the front of the counter and place his order.

"I'll take a pound of roast beef," he'd say.

That's how you make an awful shopping trip fun and memorable.

AWFUL  RELATIONSHIPS

CHAPTER TEN

ADVENTURES IN HOME ABORTIONS

A week after the *Old Lady Snuff Call* and *Click! Here Come the Cops!* incident, I recorded one of my most awful prank calls. I don't know why I kept pushing the envelope. A smart man would have interpreted my close call with the cops as a sign I should stop. But, the telemarketers kept calling and my twisted imagination kept coming up with more and more horrendous scenarios.

This prank was hardcore! My idea was to have my friend Chuck pretend to give my girlfriend a home abortion. So when the telemarketer called, I picked up, pushed record, started the call, Chuck turned on a vacuum cleaner, and my girlfriend screamed like she's in pain.

"Awwwww . . . ohhhh . . . that hurts! Oh gawwwddd!"

"Okay, I pulled out an arm, do you want me to keep going?" Chuck yells.

"Uh, finish the job, I guess," I yelled back.

I hear the telemarketer squirming. She asks, "Sir, excuse me, what's going on there? Do you want me to call back?"

"No, please keep going. My friend is just giving my girlfriend a home abortion," I say, nonchalantly. "He said he thinks he knows how to do one and I thought it would save a few bucks since the holidays are right around the corner."

You can tell by her tone she is horrified, but she stays professional and goes right back into her pitch. While she talks a hundred miles per hour, my girlfriend is screaming and my friend Chuck is yelling back at her over the blaring noise of the vacuum cleaner.

"What should I do with this leg?" Chuck yells.

"I don't know, toss it out the window for all I care," I say. "I'm sorry ma'am it's chaotic here, I missed that last part you were telling me. Can you please repeat it?"

At this point, I can tell the telemarketer is in shock but I wouldn't let up.

"I know the vacuum is loud, but my friend needs to get the rest of the pieces out," I tell her.

Finally, the telemarketer can't take it anymore and slams the phone down. The call lasted a total of three minutes.

Chuck and I start laughing uncontrollably. My girlfriend was equally amused and disgusted.

"You two are going to hell for sure!" She said.

Confess, You Fucking Creep!

Chuck and I were so pleased with the prank we took a break to go get coffee with my girlfriend. An hour later, we return to our house. The neighborhood was in chaos!

All of my neighbors were out in front of my house. My front door was busted in and there were splinters of wood all over the porch. The door was barely hanging on the hinges.

"What in the hell happened?" I asked my neighbor.

"The cops were here responding to a 911 call. No one answered the door, so they busted it down!"

Once again, I forgot the telemarketer had all of my contact information in her computer. All she had to do was call the cops and they could track me down in a few seconds.

It was more than a pair of annoyed cops that showed up this time. According to my neighbors, three cop cars had raced to the scene doing 70 in a 25 mile-per-hour zone. And, they brought an ambulance and several EMS medics because they thought a woman with a vacuum cleaner stuck in her snatch was bleeding to death.

To top it off, the lead officers were the same cops that had busted me for the *Snuff Calls* prank! Later, they tell me that they were sure it was another joke but couldn't take the chance of being wrong, so they came prepared to knock the front door down—and they did!

I felt bad I had wasted the cops' time. I decided, like an idiot, to go down to the police station and explain myself. I wanted to let them know it was a joke.

So, I drive down to the station and walk in. Guess what? The same two cops from a week before were sitting there talking about me.

"What the fuck is wrong with you?" One cop asks.

"What did I do wrong?" I say, defensively.

"You were pretending to give your girlfriend a home abortion and you don't think there's a problem with that?"

"I guess, but that telemarketer called me."

"That woman was so upset she left work early!" He says.

I can't stop myself from making a joke.

"Well, look on the bright side, I got her a half day!"

"Look," says the big cop as he hands me a form. "Fill out this statement and explain what you did. Say you're sorry because our sergeant wants to lock you up right now. He's pissed!"

"I don't know," I say, reluctantly.

"Do you realize that you could've been charged with homicide if one of our vehicles had accidentally killed someone while we were speeding to your house?"

"It's not my fault that woman believed a home abortion was being performed with a vacuum cleaner. There was no reason for her to call the cops. She did that on her own!"

At this point, I was arguing because they were scaring the shit out of me. I had never been in this kind of trouble before and didn't want to go to jail.

"Look, I promise you guys, I won't do any more prank calls! I swear!"

"Just fill out the form, say you're sorry, and you can go!" The cop says.

I was so shaken up I agreed and did what they asked. Little did I know the cops had just pulled a prank on me. Everything was about to get worse!

Law & Disorder

One of my cop friends later told me I should have never gone to the police station to admit my guilt. Pressuring me to confess on the statement was a common trick that worked in the cop's favor. Two weeks later, I received a ticket in the mail with a date for a court appearance. I was charged with disorderly contact and was facing up to six months in jail with a possible $10,000 fine. All of this over a stupid prank call. Now, I had to get a lawyer!

Luckily, my friend Tom practiced law and he agreed to represent me. He knew the prosecutor assigned to my case, and they met before the court hearing and hammered out a deal. Tom said it was worked out but I still had to go in front of the judge. The courtroom was packed but I was the second case on the docket.

"Mr. Florentine!" The judge called.

"Here, Your Honor," I responded.

"According to this complaint, you did a prank phone call and pretended your friend was giving your girlfriend a home abortion with a vacuum cleaner. The woman on the phone could hear the vacuum running and your girlfriend screaming in pain."

The whole courthouse groaned as he explained the call in detail.

"Yes, judge, I did do that."

"And, you thought that was funny?" He snapped. "You're on a show on Comedy Central and this is what you pass off as humor?"

I was biting my bottom lip so damn hard. I wanted to laugh in the judge's face. Thank God, I controlled myself!

The judge went on, "I'm giving you a fine of $750 plus another $150 for court fees. I better never see you in my court again, Mr. Florentine!"

The worst part of the whole experience was walking out past all the other people attending court. It was humiliating because everyone in the room was staring at me with a judgmental look. Now I know what a woman feels like when she has to take the walk of shame.

When I got outside, I busted out laughing. To this day, I still have the ticket they sent me in the mail. It's in a nice frame on the wall of my office. It hangs there like a badge of honor reminding me of the time I recorded the most awful and horrendous prank call I've ever imagined.

PUMPKIN-FLAVORED SHIT

I just got back from a Starbucks and the girl behind the counter asked me if I wanted a Pumpkin Spice Latte.

Nope.

I doubt there is any pumpkin in that spice latte, anyway. The "pumpkin" tastes like it must be made of really horrible chemicals made in a lab. Why would I want to drink that shit?

Most pumpkin-flavored products don't have real pumpkin! Do you know why? Because pumpkin tastes like CRAP!

Nowadays, they even have Pumpkin Spice Pringles. Why in the fuck do we need that? I haven't seen Pringles in the store since 1996. Surely, we don't need umpkin Pringles! In fact, I don't want PUMPKIN anything! STOP WITH THIS SHIT!

My good friend, Richard, loves pumpkin beer and drinks it all the time. But then again, he lives right outside of New York City and thinks the best pizza in the world is from Papa John's. Let's not trust his taste buds.

If I was a bartender and someone asked, "Can I have two pumpkin beers?"

I'd ask, "Who's the other one for?"

"One of my guy friends over there."

"NO! DRINK A BUDWEISER OR GET THE FUCK OUT!"

If pumpkin-flavored products were so good why would they just be sold seasonally and not year round? There's a reason Heineken is sold all year. It's fucking good!

Fuck pumpkin-flavored products. I don't want pumpkin spice lattes! I don't want pumpkin potato chips! I don't even want to *try* pumpkin beer. I'd rather see Hillary Clinton naked!

Part Three: Awful Relationships

You can't escape awful relationships. They're everywhere. While you're growing up you have to deal with awful family members. You get a bit older and go out into the world and make awful friends, attend awful schools, and work at awful jobs.

In your daily life, no matter how brief the relationship, you deal with awful people. Terrible drivers. Shitty servers at restaurants. Cunty cashiers and even awful corporations that scam you with bad deals and an incompetent staff. You can't go out and have a good time without getting tangled up in awful situations. This last part of the book is my take on some of my worst experiences in these awful relationships.

Awful Customer Service: Waitstaff Dummies

I'm not a narcissistic egomaniac by any means and I don't need my ass kissed when I eat out, but most of the time the service in a restaurant is atrocious. A lot of people that work in the service industry are disasters in their personal life. Alcoholics, drug addicts, bad credit, can't pay their bills, kids out of wedlock, shitty car, no insurance, and a DWI under their belt. Their personal lives are like strippers. Make cash and spend it on dumb shit the next day because more cash is coming the next night. So you're dealing with people that are hungover, high, and don't give a shit about their job and that will in turn mean bad customer service.

Worthless Waiters

Restaurants are one of the most common places you find awful customer service. Most waiters are so fucking brainless I want to stab them with my salad fork!

I went out the other night for a friend's birthday. We picked one of her favorite spots. A place she has been several times. What do you think the waitress's first question was?

"Have you guys been here before?"

"Yeah once, I came in to use the bathroom," I said.

"That's it? You just stopped in to use our toilet?" She asked.

"Why, did I clog it up?"

The waitress just stared at me dumbfounded.

Believe me, I'm just as dumbfounded that I get asked that stupid fucking question every time I go out. What is the difference? Does it matter if I've been to that restaurant before?

THEY ARE ALL THE FUCKING SAME!

You sit at a table, look at a menu, eat the food, pay your check, and leave. You do this at every restaurant in the fucking world! There is absolutely no reason to ask that stupid question unless it's a place like The Melting Pot and you need special instructions because you are cooking the food at your table.

Yeah, the food is different at different restaurants, but the process is not.

So if they ask if you've been there before, say "No, but since you're asking, it must be different from other restaurants. Do I have to go back in the kitchen and cook the food myself? If that's the case let me go get my chef hat out of my car."

Dull Waiters, Dull Knives

I eat grilled chicken every fucking day. It drives me nuts when I go to a restaurant and they don't have a sharp knife to cut the chicken.

Waiters give you those shitty butter knives that are duller than a *Big Bang Theory* episode. My toenails are sharper than those fucking knives.

When you get a steak, they bring you a sharp knife to cut your meat. Why not chicken? But, fuck no, they hand you a butter knife that can barely cut through melted butter.

I've heard waiters say the reason they don't give you a sharp knife is because chicken is supposed to be so moist that you should be able to cut through it easily. Yeah, well I've been eating chicken for thirty years, and I've never had a piece of chicken that fucking moist! Every piece of chicken I get is dryer than Betty White's snatch.

Now, whenever I ask specifically for a SHARP KNIFE they look at me like I'm an asshole and point to the butter knife that's on the table.

"That won't cut through the fucking bread roll!" I say.

I guess they think I'm crazy because when the chicken comes out the knife is always missing! So, I have to ask again.

"Can I get a sharp knife?"

"Oh, I'm sorry. I forgot it. I'll be right back!"

Now I have to wait and my chicken is getting colder and tougher to cut every second that goes by. Why didn't the waiter bring the knife when I was waiting for my fucking food? They had a whole thirty minutes to get the table organized. I want to stab the waiter with the butter knife but I know it won't break his skin.

Prep the Fucking Table

Do a little prep work if you're a server, okay?

If you have hamburgers and French fries on the menu, people who order it will want ketchup. Put it on the table before the order comes out. It's pretty simple.

Some asshole will want more salt on their already salty fries. Make sure salt and pepper are on the fucking table. Do it while your customers are waiting for their food. Otherwise, they'll ask for it when the food comes out.

If I were the waiter, I would ask if the table needs anything. Extra napkins? Steak sauce? An extra plate? I wouldn't ask if the meal is okay ten seconds after it arrives at the table. I don't know how it is yet I'm not finished chewing my first piece yet! Come back halfway through the meal and check in? Either way, who cares if it's the meal of the century or not. I'll have another one in six hours. I eat three meals a day. Sometimes one is bad but there's another one on the way soon. I'm eating at a chain restaurant so it's most likely going to be a shitty meal so who gives a fuck?

Plain Stupidity

Here's another annoyance, when you go out for breakfast it's impossible to order a plain egg-white omelet. I have a problem with this every fucking time!

"What would you like to order, sir?" The waitress asks.

"Can I get a plain egg-white omelet, please?"

"Okay, what do you want in the omelet?" She asks.

"Eggs!"

There is always complete silence after that answer.

"Sir, you don't have to be rude."

"I'm not being rude. I want eggs in my PLAIN omelet."

"What else?" She asks.

"I said plain. Plain means plain, right? When you order a plain bagel, does it come out with fucking jelly on it? No, it's just fucking plain."

I guess the idea of a plain egg-white omelet is incomprehensible. It's especially confusing to waiters in a small town.

"The cook said he can't separate the eggs," they say.

"Really? It takes exactly two seconds."

"Sir, we don't do that here!"

Sometimes when I ask for a plain omelet they ask me, "Do you want cheese in that?"

I refuse to answer that question and sit there in silence.

"Sir, excuse me, do you want cheese in your omelet?"

"Did I ask for cheese?"

"No, you didn't."

"Okay, so why are we talking about cheese?"

"You just want the omelet plain with nothing in it?"

"I want the eggs in it."

"Obviously, you want the eggs. I asked if you wanted cheese because most people like cheese."

"Most people like to go on vacations but there are people that don't."

"Sir, that makes no sense."

"Neither does your theory about cheese, you fucking retard!"

Room for Disaster

Another thing that annoys the fuck out of me is the question the waiter asks after dinner, "Did you save any room for dessert?"

I don't know how to save room for dessert. I don't have little men in my stomach moving the food around to make extra room. I'm not nine years old. I don't eat desserts anymore. I just had three glasses of wine, I'm not going to ruin my buzz with a piece of chocolate fucking cake. You don't mix icing with alcohol. That's a recipe for disaster!

I went out to dinner with my guy friend the other night and he ordered two pieces of cake.

"Two?" I asked.

"I can't help it! I have a sweet tooth," he said.

"No, you don't. You're forty years old, you don't have a fucking sweet tooth. You're overeating because you are depressed that you're in a bad marriage."

"Why would you say that?" He asked.

"You just texted your wife and called her a cunt!" I pointed to his phone.

"Yeah but I put a *smiley face* at the end!"

"Perfect, let me know how that works out for you motherfucker!"

Awful Stores: Big-Box Scams

Restaurants are bad but big-box stores like Sam's Club and Costco are FUCKING AWFUL! People who swear by them act like they're in a cult. They won't shop anywhere else and don't understand people who might have a different opinion.

"You don't go to Costco? Fucking Costco is AMAZING! It's an event when I go!"

If you think going to Costco on a Saturday afternoon is an event, you have a sad life. These stores are nothing but scams!

Try a Sample of Shit

First, the con men running these awful warehouses lure you in with shitty food!

My friend said, "I like it because they put out samples. I can eat lunch there because around every corner there's free food! You might as well try it all. Who doesn't like free stuff?"

I don't like free stuff when they're doing a promotion somewhere and they're giving out free T-shirts, I don't take it just because it's free. Sorry, I'm not going to wear a *Bud Light Lime* T-shirt that's so big it hangs down to my fucking ankles.

Just because it's free doesn't mean it's edible. It's fucking garbage—a greasy piece of a hot dog or an awful-looking sausage.

I wish I could set up a sample table in Costco. I would collect a bunch of dog shit, pack it in bulk, and put it on display.

"Here's a dried piece of dog shit! Take it, it's free! It doesn't cost you anything! Mmmmm!"

People in these stores are buying junk food in bulk. They put horrible crap in their mouths all the time. I have no doubt, they'll love dog shit on a toothpick!

Fucked by a Fuel Pump

When you shop at big-box stores, you waste money on gas because you aren't driving to the free and convenient supermarket a mile from your house. The nearest Costco is nine miles away so that's an eighteen-mile round-trip. Now, you're spending more on gas to save money. It doesn't make any fucking sense!

Guess what, they've thought of this, too. Big-box stores now sell their own gas. Another way they swindle people into thinking they're getting a deal.

There's a Costco a few miles from my house and I go by it every day. They charge $2.31 a gallon. There's a 7-11 a mile away that sells gas for the same price. The gas line at Costco is always twenty cars long. 7-11 never has a wait. You can pull right up to the pump and be in and out in three minutes. Meanwhile, the Costco cult members are wasting fuel by idling fifteen minutes to fill up their tanks with the precious Costco gas.

It is true that Costco gas is cheaper than Exxon. But, Exxon inflates their price because people think its better quality gas. That's another scam. Gas is the same wherever you get it.

Also, you don't need premium for twenty-five cents more. That's all bullshit! They've done studies that prove it doesn't matter what you put in your tank since newer cars are built different from the shitty cars our parents drove. It's not 1973! I've never been in someone's car and said, "Wow, this car rides smooth, you must have put Exxon Premium in your tank!" If Costco cultists did some research instead of dreaming about the dog shit samples they'll eat this weekend—they might actually save some fucking money!

Shitty Costco Clothes

They sell clothes at Costco, too. They're supposed to be designer clothes but it might be a good idea to look a little closer. I'm sure those Calvin Klein jeans are the fuck-ups from the sweatshop where the pocket or the zipper is a little off and the guy who bought them can't zip up his pants.

Don't brag you got your clothes at a fucking bulk store. There's nothing more white trash. I'd have more respect for you if you stole clothes from that charity bin in the fucking parking lot.

Check Out Anytime, but Never Leave!

The worst thing at Costco is the thirty-minute wait at the register thanks to the assholes with endless shit crammed in their huge carts. After you get rung up, you have to wait again for the old retarded guy at the door. He's ninety years old and they are making him check your receipt and your cart for hidden items! He marks each item one by one and that takes another fifteen minutes. If you're spending $50 a year on a membership you have money to buy tons of awful shit!

By the time the old fuck checks your receipt you've spent forty-five minutes from the checkout counter to the car. Then the parking lot is completely packed because all the assholes in a ten-mile radius go to Costco at the same time to get their free samples!

Outside, you have six cars following you hoping to take your parking spot. God forbid they park in the outer lot where there are plenty of open spots. They're going to walk three miles up and down those fucking aisles but won't walk an extra thirty feet from their car to the door? So, now I feel like I'm getting stalked while these lazy cocksuckers in their cars watch my every move!

So now, there's pressure to throw your stuff in the car and pull out quickly because six assholes, in gas-guzzling SUVs, are waiting for your parking spot.

It took so long to get out of the store you need to chill for a second.

Meanwhile, there's a car on each side and you don't know which way to pull out because these assholes refuse to walk a few extra yards. They want to rush into the store so they can eat free pieces of shit on a toothpick. Fuck you! I'm taking a nap in the front seat before I pull out. How about that, jerk-offs?

Scams in Bulk

Another part of the big-box store scam is the shopping bag policy. There are no bags!

When you get out to your car, you have to put each product one by one into the back. It's a huge pain in the ass. As soon as you pull away, it sounds like a fucking bowling alley in the trunk. Shit is flying all over the place at every turn. When you get home, half the stuff is broken. Well, at least you have broken glass in bulk now!

These big-bulk stores make you pay for a membership if you want to shop in their stores. This is another ingenious part of the fraud. The cheapest plan those stores offer is around $50 a year. They want you to feel like it's a special privilege being a member.

If you break it down, you're being ripped off financially. Let's say before you joined the store you went shopping once every two weeks. You buy the membership so you can buy everything in bulk. You think this is great because you will only have to go shopping once per month.

During your first shopping trip, you buy shit like eighty-pound bags of oranges to make sure you are stocked up. You calculate that you will shop twelve times a year. But, then you realize you're in the hole because of the $50 membership fee. That means you need to save $4.16 per trip just to break even for the year.

Also, you have to factor in storage costs. You need to buy an extra refrigerator to store all the big shit you're buying. The shittiest refrigerator will run you at least $400, plus you have to pay for the extra electricity you use to run it each month. So far, all you've done is spend more money than you did before!

Researching the Racket

Everyone believes that the cheap prices make up for the extra up-front costs. So, I recently snuck into a Costco to do research on prices. Gift cards are one of their most popular items. Wait until you hear the deals on these!

They had a $25 *Starbucks* gift card for $24.64! Can you believe how cheap that is? You are saving thirty-six cents! The *AMC Movie Theater* $30 gift card is a whopping fifty-two cents off at $29.48! HOLY FUCK!

Why isn't everyone in America talking about these great gift card deals? This should be on the national news! The crawl on the bottom on CNN should say *Go to Costco and save $0.52 on a $30 gift card!* Here are more amazing bargains I found:

100-Pack of Blank CDs for $17.97
Who the fuck uses blank CDs anymore and why would you need a hundred of them? Maybe once a year you might need to burn something onto a blank CD. Go to Staples and buy a three pack for $2.49. That pack will last you twenty years and save you $15.48 and $2 in gas.

4-Pack of Extra-Large Rolls of Duct Tape for $6
Unless you're a serial killer who is taping up body parts every night, you won't use up a four-pack of extra-large duct tape in your lifetime.

24-Pack of Yellow Highlighters for $9
You'll only use twenty-four highlighters if you need to highlight every fucking word in *War and Peace*. I don't care if you're a teacher for fucking thirty years you still don't need that many highlighters!

72-Pack of Pencils for $7
Seventy-two pencils for the low, low price of $7! No one has a pencil sharpener in the house anymore. Unless you're using the pencils for firewood that deal fucking stinks!

Count the Ways You're Conned

The regular supermarkets have started selling bulk items, too. They've figured out the scam and now they are selling things with comparable prices. The ShopRite by my house has a 32-pack of toilet paper just like Costco. They have huge bags of snacks, spinach in massive containers, and oversized packages of fucking lettuce!

It's true you can only get the 60-pack of toothpaste at Costco but why do we need that much? Just buy it when you run out. It's not that big of a deal. It's what you do in life. You make trips to the super-market to get fresh milk, eggs, and orange juice.

Assholes who belong to the Costco cult will say, "I stock up on my milk by buying five gallons at a time!"

What they don't tell you is they wind up pouring the last three gallons down the drain because it's expired and it starts a fight in the relationship because someone is bitching that you're wasting food and money.

Just because it's in bulk doesn't mean it's a good deal. The club members are brainwashed so much it's like talking to a woman whose husband beats her. You try to get her to leave and she's says, "Yeah, but he's a good father." Yeah, he's a good puncher too.

If you don't factor in the consequences of buying absurd shit like a forty-pound watermelon you deserve to lose money! It is so damn heavy they had to use a forklift to put it in your trunk. With the extra weight in the car it lowers your MPG so it's costing you another $2 in wasted gas to get home. When you get there, you have to ask the neighbor to help you lift your huge watermelon out of your trunk. If he's black he's going to think you're a racist.

It's impossible to eat more than six pounds of watermelon before it goes bad and you have to throw most of it away. You spend $26 on the damn thing thinking you're getting a deal but you can only eat a fifth of it. Do the math—YOU JUST GOT FUCKED OVER!

When people shop at these places with the mindset that every-thing in the store is a deal they spend more money and buy more shit than they need.

They see a 6,000-pack of printer paper for $22 and buy it because it is a great price. Meanwhile they use a printer every few months to print a one-page boarding pass for their airplane ticket. They make a joke about it when they realize how fucking stupid they've been,

"Well, at least we know we won't run out of paper, ha ha!" Yeah, that's fucking hilarious!

Count the ways you've been conned. One, you were fucked on the membership fee. Two, you were fucked by the no bags and broken glass situation. Three, you were fucked on the storage costs. Four, the clothes are unwearable. Five, the gas is a scam. You need a new refrigerator. The food is shit and half of what you buy goes to waste. You spent more than you ever did before! At this point, I say you've been FUCKED IN BULK!

CHAPTER ELEVEN

MEET THE CREEPS

You would think my court date for *Adventures in Home Abortions* would have been the end of me getting in trouble with the law, but no, cops were becoming a regular part of my comedy career. These brushes with the legal system just inspired me to keep going.

In fact, I made the leap from audio to video and produced a series of hidden-camera prank shows called *Meet the Creeps* with my friend Don Jamieson. The premise of the show was simple—turn on a hidden camera and fuck with people. *Meet the Creeps* ended up being popular enough to produce three volumes and do a pilot for Comedy Central that didn't get picked up because they thought it was too mean-spirited. Our style was brutal. There were no happy endings during our sketches. The bit ends and then it fades to black and you're thinking, *What the fuck just happened?*

How Not to Dump a Dead Body

While we were producing *Meet the Creeps,* Don and I visited my brother at one of his construction sites. He's in real estate and was building some new condominiums. While we took the tour, we noticed an over-sized dumpster set up in front of the worksite. That gave us one of our more twisted ideas—a bit we called *Dead Body.*

Construction workers are possessive with the dumpster and are instantly annoyed when anyone uses it. They get pissed when people throw away small things like coffee cups. They only want demolition trash thrown in there and are always watching out for people who might misuse it. We figured this made them perfect marks for our next prank.

On the day of filming, we rolled our friend Chuck up in a carpet, stuffed him in the car, and drove over to the construction site. The idea was to dump our fake body in full sight of the construction guys and secretly film their reactions.

We pulled our car up and started to offload our deceased buddy. That's when we learned our first lesson about dumping the dead. Always be able to lift the corpse you're trying to dump!

Chuck was too damn heavy! Don and I barely got him out of the car. Once we dragged his ass to the dumpster, we couldn't lift him high enough to toss him inside. That's when one of the construction workers confronted us.

"HEY! What are you guys doing?"

"Oh, hey man. We're just getting rid of this old carpet," Don said.

The worker wasn't pleased. Before he could say another word, we dropped Chuck and ran back to the car.

Driving away was Chuck's cue to wiggle and scream for help. Our job was to drive around the block, wait a few minutes, and then come back and pretend to ask for directions so our hidden camera could capture their reactions. As soon as Chuck screamed, another construction worker sprang into action. He ran over and cut open the carpet to free our fake victim.

"HOLY SHIT! WHERE AM I?" Chuck yelled.

"What in the fuck?" The worker said.

"THOSE GUYS KIDNAPPED ME!"

"What the hell happened?"

"Last thing I remember, I was in a gay bar having a great night. Then, I wake up inside this fucking carpet!"

"Okay, calm down man."

"They must have DRUGGED ME! I don't know what the hell happened!" Chuck said.

"Stay right here, let me get some help!"

This happened so fast Chuck forgot to signal us. We were around the corner waiting for his text. We never got the text but we did get an anxious call. The cops were there, they had Chuck, and they wanted to speak to us!

Apparently, this old fuck that lived across the street had watched the whole thing. He didn't know it was a prank and called the police. We found three cop cars flashing their blue lights when we pulled back up to the dumpster. It looked like a real crime scene. A pair of them confronted me immediately. This wasn't bad cop, good cop, it was young cop, and old cop. The old cop was pissed!

"Tell me what the fuck is going on here?" He yelled.

"It was just a joke," I said.

"A JOKE? You think this is a joke?"

Before I could answer, the younger officer asked me my name.

"Oh, I know who you are!" Young Cop said.

"I don't give a shit who he is," Old Cop said. "This isn't a fucking joke! Do you read the paper, Mr. Florentine?"

"Only the sports page." I couldn't help but be a wiseass. The old cop looked at me like he wanted to punch me in the fucking face.

"Well, if you did read the paper, you'd know one week ago someone left a REAL MURDER VICTIM in a dumpster RIGHT DOWN THE STREET! We've been on the lookout ever since!"

"We had no idea!" I pretended to be shocked, but I was thinking, *How the fuck would I know that?*

The old cop then tells me he's not going to let this one slide. "I don't care if this was a joke. You're getting charged with something!"

"Let me talk to these guys." The young cop pulls us aside. "Dude, so you're the Jim Florentine from *Crank Yankers* and *Howard Stern*? I didn't want to laugh in my sergeant's face but this is fucking hilarious! Do you have any of those *Terrorizing Telemarketers* CDs on you?"

"Yeah, I have a bunch in my car. Why?"

"I want to get a few of those from you but first we need to calm down my boss." He was having trouble keeping a straight face. "Holy shit, this is funny but I'm going to pretend I'm mad at you. So play along!"

After the young cop gave us a fake lecture, he talked to the old cop about dropping the charges and he reluctantly agreed.

We were lucky this police officer had a sense of humor. You can watch *Dumping Dead Body* on *Meet the Creeps* videos if you're interested. Don remembers that day well! Chuck was so heavy that Don threw his back out and was in bed for a week!

FUCK THE FALL SEASON

Fuck the fall! I don't like it! Yeah, I know people think the leaves are nice to look at but I hate those fuckers. After they change colors, they fall off the trees. Who gives a fuck that leaves change colors? It's the same colors every year. It's not like we suddenly have new colors to get excited about. I have a big yard so I end up spending all my time raking leaves! IT SUCKS!

Also, it gets cold and I have to use my fireplace. That puts me out in the yard chopping wood and constantly lugging wood into the house to feed the fire. Nothing about that is fun!

Then, it gets dark in the afternoon. Why in the fuck do we still have a time change? There's no logical reason! It only benefits the electrical company. They make more money because you put your lights on earlier. It seems like the day is over before it even fucking starts.

All of that convinces me there's nothing good about the fall. Plus, women start wearing more clothes. They put away their summer outfits and start wrapping up. I think some of these women wear seventeen fucking layers. Any season that has women putting away the yoga pants and dressing like mummies means it's awful! By the time I take get all those layers off and get her naked I've lost my erection and need to take a nap!

Awful Relationships: DJ Disasters

Awful relationships seem to get worse the moment people get married. If you're an awful person you will plan an awful wedding!

I know this because I was a wedding DJ before I became a comedian. That job only lasted about six months because I was one of the worst DJs ever. I wouldn't play requests and I was just plain rude. For instance, I refused to play the Kool & The Gang song "Celebration." I wouldn't even buy a copy of it. People would come up and request it and I would refuse!

"Why would I have that song? It fucking stinks! What else do you want to hear?"

There's no reason to play "Celebration" ever again. We get it, we're at a wedding and it's a celebration so it makes sense to play a song with the same title. That fucking song should be retired because it is so stale but, like many terrible songs, bad wedding DJs keep it alive.

Most wedding DJs are lazy fucks. They use the same tricks at every wedding. They play songs like "Celebration" after dinner to get everyone on the dance floor. Sometimes they mix it up and play that horrendous Sister Sledge song "We Are Family." They think it's a good choice since two families have been brought together into one big clan. *We are family*, you get it? I'd rather get AIDS! No one has ever walked away from a wedding thinking, *I can't believe "Celebration" wasn't played.*

One time, a guy requested that I play "Hot, Hot, Hot" by Buster Poindexter. That song is ABSOLUTE SHIT! I asked him how old he was and made him go back to his table.

On several occasions, I put Metallica songs on when the wedding party was eating dinner. I did it so they would eat faster. One groom, who hated the song, came over and confronted me.

"Hey, what are you playing?"

"Don't worry about it, just hurry up and eat so I can get the fuck out of here!" I said.

"Look at the guests, they don't seem happy about it either." He yelled.

"The reason they look miserable is because they're eating shitty food! Nobody wants almonds in their green beans, asshole!"

Needless to say, that was one of my last weddings.

Guests would also ask me to play the fucking Chicken Dance and they wanted me to go out on the dance floor and lead the dance. That was never going to happen. I would always find a couple of drunken cornballs to do it so I didn't have to embarrass myself.

When I compared myself to other wedding DJs, it was obvious I needed to find another gig. I hated most of the song requests. I didn't like leading the stupid fucking traditions, and I didn't bring props to the gigs. Some cornball DJs will get on the dance floor with a wig and inflatable guitar and play "You Shook Me All Night Long." People think it's funny and that it will get the party started. There's nothing fun about that, and it won't get the party started. You want to get the party started? Have a couple of girls start blowing guys on the dance floor. That's how you start a party!

There are many songs that have been played to death. I've had enough of Neil Diamond's song "Sweet Caroline." When it comes on all the drunks in the room who can't sing make it even more miserable. White-trash guys put their arms around each other, sing loud as fuck, and reminisce about the cool parties they had in their twenties.

They get emotional because now they're older and too busy to party or see each other. They say it brings back good memories. To me, it seems like an excuse to watch a bunch of assholes make even bigger assholes out of themselves.

"We use to sing this at every fucking party," they say.

Wow! That sounds like it was a fucking blast! I wish I had gone to your college! I didn't put my arms around guys and sing songs at my college parties. Most nights, I was on the bathroom floor fucking a fatty!

Playing hip-hop music at white-trash weddings is another questionable experiment. I knew I had to quit when brides demanded I do this! If you're wedding is in a VFW hall, in the middle of South Jersey, and Sterno cans are heating the fucking food, you don't play hip-hop music! That's a bad fucking mix!

The bride has daddy issues. We get it. You're rebelling against your dad. He grew up on classic rock and but now you're mad at him, and to piss him off you blast Drake at the wedding he's financing. Ungrateful cunt!

Wedding DJs do it anyway. They think they can get away with playing safe hip-hop songs like "I Got a Feeling" by the Black Eyed Peas. That song stinks.

I got a feeling this marriage won't work out. I got a feeling this wedding is a disaster. I got a feeling half the bridesmaids will be crying at the end of the night because they can't handle their alcohol. I got a feeling there will be a fistfight between two men because they can't handle their booze, either. I got a feeling I'm going to shit myself on the way home because I had almonds in my green beans.

THAT'S THE FEELING I GOT!

Your Awful Wedding

Try to consider your friends when you plan your fucking wedding. Don't make it too expensive and don't make it stupid! Many years ago, I got a call from my buddy asking me to be in his wedding.

He said, "Hey, man I want you to be a groomsman but here's the deal, you have to rent a hat and cane! Don't worry all the groomsmen will wear the same thing."

I said, "The only way I'm getting a hat and cane is if I can shit in the hat and wrap the cane around your fucking neck."

He didn't like that response but he got my point. I'd rather wear a hat full of shit than go to another awful wedding! Any wedding full of assholes twirling canes is going to be brutal.

If you're thinking about inviting me to a wedding, don't do it! I don't want to be in your wedding party. I don't want to buy a tuxedo or wear a fucking bow tie. And, I'm not renting any stupid shit like a cummerbund, top hat, or tails.

In fact, let's ban tuxedos at weddings. Stop making people waste hundreds of dollars on something they'll wear one time.

Of course, people look better in a tux, but who cares? Rocky Dennis, the deformed kid from the movie *Mask*, looks better in a tux. A tux changes him from a one to four on a scale of one to ten, but it's still not worth it.

If you're the best man, you're forced to get a tux. That's one reason I figured out a way to avoid being the best man in the future.

Friend: "Hey man, will you be my best man at my wedding?"

You: "I'd love to but I have to tell you something first. I was drunk one night and ate your fiancé's box. You still want me to be your best man? No? I didn't think so!"

NICE! I destroyed a relationship and saved myself a grand.

Even if you're not in the wedding party you still have to wear a fucking suit. I only have one suit and when I bought it I made sure it could be worn in February or July. I need to be able to wear it in a snowstorm and a heat wave. I don't want to hear shit from a girl who says it's not the right color for a certain time of year. I don't give a fuck. I've worn it five times in the last four years. The last time I wore it I found a roll in my suit pocket from the wedding before. It was still kind of fresh so I put it in the microwave and ate it.

Awful Person, Awful Plans

How and when you plan the wedding shows whether you are an awful person. For instance, never plan a wedding on a Sunday during football season! My comic friend Bob Levy, whom I love, did that one time. I was so fucking irritated I would miss the Dolphins game I brought a portable TV to the celebration, and I was in the fucking wedding party!

At one point, the planner had the wedding party line up for introductions. When they announced my name, I didn't acknowledge the crowd because I was glued to the screen as I walked out on my intro. The Dolphins were about to score and I wasn't missing it!

I even had that TV with me on the dance floor while I was forced to dance with one of the bridesmaids. It must have looked ridiculous to see me out there with that super long antenna waving around and me watching the game over the woman's shoulder.

Even though I was watching the game, my dick was paying attention. I managed to get a hard-on because it was a long slow dance. That was a strange experience. I've never had an erection watching an NFL game before. I'm still not sure if it was rubbing on my dance partner or the sight of Dan Marino's ass!

Douchebags in the wedding party love to wear sunglasses when they are introduced. These jerk-offs put the *Men in Black* sunglasses on and do a dance from that shitty movie from twenty years ago. Will Smith stinks and so does that movie. Most of the people don't even get their joke. They are turning to each other saying, "Why are they wearing sunglasses indoors?"

I also hate that rehearsed little dance the wedding party does when they walk out. No one is thinking, *Wow, I wonder what the next couple will do? This is going to be crazy. Oh, look the guy put his hands in the air and the girl shook her butt. This wedding is fun.*

Everything about it reeks of desperation. They actually rehearsed that corny shit. Yuck! A bomb threat would be perfect for that moment when the wedding party is being introduced. They'd need to evacuate the building for a while and it would ruin that silly idea. Hopefully, their sunglasses would get trampled on the way out.

Catholic Mess

Here's more advice: don't have a Catholic Mass wedding! They are way too long and extremely boring.

At least make it interesting if you do. I was the best man at my brother's wedding and when it was time to pull out the ring at the altar I handed him a glass stink bomb instead. His wife was so disgusted!

The only break you get is communion. But, to receive communion you have to clean your slate of sins and go to church every week. It's funny how no one gives a shit about that if it's a wedding. Eighty percent of the people go up to receive it whether they should or not.

During the last Catholic wedding I attended, I saw a guy who had just cheated on his wife go up and receive communion. A stripper gave him a blowjob at the bachelor party the night before and he was in line to receive the holy sacrament six hours later. I don't think he had time to confess that sin let alone wash his mule off before he put his tux on.

Maybe people go up because the fucking service is so long. Everyone is hung-over and starving. Might as well take the snack the priest is offering! It will be a long fucking time before we eat! I'm sure some priests love the moment when a guy is about to receive communion and has his mouth open and tongue out.

Destination Weddings

The worst wedding is a destination wedding. Planning this kind of wedding is completely selfish! If you book a destination wedding, you're a cunt.

If you insist on doing it, don't invite anybody but your family. It's $1,500 for plane tickets for two to St. Martin. Don't get mad when your friends don't show. I'm not going! Why would I travel that far to watch you both say "I do"? If both of you get on that plane and go, I have a feeling you'll both say yes. No need for me to be there. Film it on your iPhone and send it to me. I'll pretend that I watched it and tell you it looked great. Then, have a big party when you come back home. I'm not wasting my only vacation week of the year to watch you two get married when I know damn well six months later one of you will be sleeping on my couch because your marriage is falling apart already.

When I got married I had a destination wedding. The destination was the VFW hall down the street. Maybe that's why my marriage was over in two years.

I hate when brides declare their wedding day My Day! No, it's not. You just picked a day on the calendar that worked for both of you. You rented a church or a hall on that specific day. That's all you did.

"No, this is my day!" They say.

Is it really your day?

"Yeah, it's my day. It's Nikki's day today!"

"Really? I was watching CNN today and I didn't see that scroll across the bottom of the screen. If it was, they would have announced it—today is Nikki's day because she found some fat guy to marry her!"

Cash Bar Backfire

Even if you go to a regular wedding, you spend a lot of money. They should itemize the costs on the fucking invitations. It sets you back at least a grand even if you're not in the wedding party.

There are other hidden expenses like the gift money in the card, the hotel room, and whatever your date's dress cost. A woman has to buy a new dress for every wedding no matter what.

You try to talk logic to her but it never works.

"Just wear the dress you wore to the last wedding, no one will know."

"Yeah, but I'll know."

"No one from that last wedding will be at this one. No one will know, I promise!"

"Someone might find out."

"Can't you keep a secret? We had anal sex last night. Are you going to go around and tell everyone that secret? I mean, I already told my friends but I'm sure you can keep it under wraps."

Here's another thing that sucks—weddings with cash bars! If you have a cash bar, you're a STINGY CUNT! I have to spend money to go to your dumb wedding and you make me pay for drinks?

In that case, I'll pay for my drinks with the cash I put in your card. When I need a new round, I'll open your gift card and take it from there. And because you had a shitty cash bar, I'm giving the bartender a huge tip every fucking time he pours me a new one!

Useless Wedding Gifts

Buying wedding gifts is another thing that sucks! The list of things that married couples ask for is a fucking nightmare. I don't give a fuck if somebody needs a Crock-Pot. I'll never look at another wedding registry unless it's posted on the YouPorn homepage.

My solution is to give couples cash. Only chicks want gifts. How about I give you the cash and you go get the fucking gift? The last wedding I attended was for my male friend who is a fucking alcoholic and a gambler. I know that he'll be happier with $300 bucks in an envelope than a salad bowl that he'll never use!

That's what a guy wants to open up on his wedding night—a salad bowl. He'd much rather open his wife's ass cheeks and toss her salad.

Women really need to stop with the damn kitchen appliances. They want shit they don't need like blenders, steamers, and toaster ovens. One time, I tried to reason with my ex-wife about needing a toaster.

"Hey baby, we don't need a toaster, we never eat toast," I said.

"Yeah, but we need it just in case people stay over," she said.

The truth was we'd been living in a fucking condo for three years. Never had any guests except for one guy who stayed over because he was so fucking hammered. The next morning he didn't ask for toast, he was in the bathroom puking his guts out while the toaster oven collected dust on the counter.

No one ever said, "I would take you up on the offer to stay but I know you won't have toast for me in the morning."

If you really want a gift that bad go buy it your fucking self!

BLACK FRIDAY SHOPPERS

On Black Friday, I hope no one gets up early. You are an idiot if you think you will get a $19 television by waiting in the freezing weather with three hundred other assholes.

IT'S NOT GOING TO HAPPEN!

They are only giving away one TV for that price. The first person that gets in runs straight to the electronics department and gets that TV. No one else does.

Black Friday is out of control. Every year these idiotic crowds trample someone to death. Do you really want to be that person? Do you really want to be known as the asshole that lost his life trying to save $20 on an iPad?

How do you think your family will feel? They'll have to live with that shame the rest of their lives. Imagine your siblings trying to explain that idiocy.

"Yeah, I had a brother once but he died."

"I'm sorry to hear that. What happened?"

"Well, he got trampled to death."

"That's fucking horrible! Was he trying to escape a burning building or something?"

"No, he died outside a Walmart at six in the morning trying to save $3 on an iPhone case."

Rest in peace, retard!

Vows That Don't Suck

The costs of weddings are bad enough. The stupid traditions are even worse. For instance, couples that write their own wedding vows are a fucking embarrassment! I heard my guy friend say in his vows he knew his wife was "the one" the first time he saw her.

NO, HE DIDN'T!

If that were true, he wouldn't have waited four years, only to break down after she pressured him into the engagement.

He saw his wife for the very first time in a bar, and I was with him, and he said, and I quote, "Who is that chick with the big tits?" You didn't buy her a ring that night, you ordered her the strongest drink possible. You didn't want to get engaged, you wanted to get her loose so you could get a blowjob in the bar parking lot!

All her dumb friends were getting married so it put even more pressure on you. So, if you're going to write your own vows, be honest.

Hey honey, you know we're here today because you pressured the shit out of me to get married! Last year, I took you to Cancun on vacation. I couldn't top that when your next birthday came up. I knew a sweater wouldn't work this time. Then, your job offered free health insurance for families, and since I'll need back surgery soon, I bought you this ring! With this ring, and under a fucking ton of pressure, I thee wed!

Now, that's a TRUTHFUL wedding vow!

Cake Madness

Enough with the fucking wedding cakes! Nobody walks away from
a wedding talking about how the cake tasted. I've been to forty-two
weddings and nobody was raving about the cake the next day. So,
there's no reason to waste time on taste tests while you're planning
the wedding. I don't even want to taste the cake that's sitting on our
kitchen counter three inches away from me. Cakes taste the same at
a wedding or a kid's Chuck E. Cheese birthday party.

My ex-wife wanted me to drive three hours on a football Sunday
to taste cakes for the wedding. I wouldn't drive that far for a threesome let alone for something that I stopped eating when I was five
years old. Cake is for kids. If you're an adult and you still like cake you
have some underlying issues that are unresolved from childhood.
Cake should be an afterthought once you're an adult. It's almost like
when someone offers you a shot in the bar. You're like, "Ok, I guess
I'll have it since everyone else is having one."

Also, the cake is always served about three hours after the wedding
begins. That's the time everyone is drunk. Do you really think your
guests will care if the cake tastes good after doing five shots of whiskey?
You could serve dog shit and people wouldn't notice the difference.

Then eventually the DJ fires up that awful "The Bride Cuts the
Cake" song. At this point in the night, nobody gives a shit about the
cutting of the cake but we're forced to endure it.

I'm trying to pick up the maid of honor and I have a soggy six in
my pants from slow dancing with her. Now, I have to watch people
cut a cake? I already know how to cut a fucking cake!

I think the whole cake thing is stupid as fuck but there are guests
that want to see if the bride and groom feed each other. The groom
weighs 450 pounds. I have a feeling his mouth is going to be wide
open during the cake feeding.

"Oh, isn't that so cute! Did he just smear cake on her face? Oh,
my goodness, isn't this a fun wedding."

NO, THERE'S NOTHING FUN ABOUT THAT.

I wish the groom would take the whole cake and dump it on his bride's head. "That's for asking me to taste test this shitty cake and miss football Sunday!"

Freezer Burn

There is a dumb superstition with a wedding cake, too. Couples save a portion of the cake and keep it in their freezer until their first anniversary. It's meant to be good luck for the marriage. You know what's good luck? Your wife gets a personal trainer and she doesn't fuck him. You know what else is good luck? You hire a good-looking nanny and your husband doesn't fuck her.

If the cake tasted like shit at the wedding, how bad will it be a year later when it has freezer burn?

Eating a piece of the cake a year later has nothing to do with the future of your marriage. Imagine if one of your friends started having marriage problems and had to come over and sleep on your couch, even though you didn't have toast for him in the morning.

"What happened to your marriage? You guys were always so happy!"

"We were getting along great but we forgot to eat our frozen wedding cake on our anniversary and things started to go downhill from there!"

If he really believed that stupid shit, I'd put him out of his misery by smothering him with a pillow.

Cock-Blockers on Crack

Another dumb tradition is having kids take part in the wedding. Kids shouldn't be allowed at weddings because they ruin it for the adults. They get cake in their system and run around the dance floor like they're on crack.

I'm on the dance floor grinding on my date and I have a four-year-old wrapped around my ankle. Get them the fuck out off the dance floor! I have to punt him across the room.

Weddings should be an adults-only zone. There's enough shit for kids everywhere else. Can we have one day without them around?

Some adult shit is about to go down. I have my date in the bathroom stall and some guy is changing his kid's shitty diaper a foot from me. It is tough to keep an erection when you have some douchebag dad talking baby talk next to you. You already dropped a grand on the wedding. Drop another hundred on a babysitter. YOU CHEAP FUCK!

Caught on Camera

In the past, couples would put out disposable cameras so guests would take candid photos of the celebration. That may be the one good tradition at weddings. I seriously miss those cameras! As soon as my friends got one we went in the bathroom and took pictures of our penises, balls, and assholes. If we had to drop a deuce we took pictures of that, too. Then, we turned in the cameras like nothing happened.

After one of my friend's weddings, this backfired. He was in a rage when he got back from his honeymoon. Apparently, his new mother-in-law was tasked with developing all the film, and that didn't go well.

"I can't believe you fucking guys did that!" He yelled. "My mother-in-law was disgusted by those pictures!"

He didn't talk to any of us for over a year.

A similar thing happened when I was in my close friend's wedding party. One guy took a picture of his dick and left the camera on the table for the family. The groom's mother got it developed and sees the penis and fucking flips out.

"This has to be Jim Florentine," she said. "None of the other men would do something so disgraceful!"

When my friend returned from his honeymoon, his mother confronted him with the picture and her theory about me being the culprit. He analyzed the picture and noticed that the guilty man was wearing a suit.

"It can't be Florentine. He wore a tuxedo during the ceremony because he was in the wedding party."

Later, he did more detective work and found out the guilty party was a cousin of his. He was a married doctor who had three kids.

Here's another story like that one. My ex-girlfriend's brother had a great job as a hotel general manager. He heard about my antics with the throwaway cameras and thought it was funny. At his Christmas office party, he decided to have his friend take a picture of his dick in the bathroom. Problem was they took the picture wrong and got his face in the picture too. When the pictures were developed he lost his six-figure job, all because of my childish behavior. Maybe weddings are good for something.

Hair Up, Hard-on Down

Why do the bride and the chicks in the wedding party all put their hair up in a ponytail or a bun on the wedding day? Stop doing that.

Girls never look good with their hair up. In fact, they look terrible! You've got big fucking Dumbo ears. Those ears are usually covered up so they are super pale. They don't match the rest of your tan. Always remember, there isn't a single chick with nice ears. No guy ever dated a chick because of her ears unless she couldn't hear out of them and he can say whatever he wants to her. Women spend $300 on makeup and fucking hair dye so they don't have any roots. You girls did all of that shit yet you fucking twirl it up in a bun so everybody can see what your mediocre face looks like?

You go down three notches when your hair's up. Any girl who's a nine and puts their hair up slides down to a six. If you're a seven, now you're a four. You waited your whole life for this day and you look like shit. The only time a chick should put her hair up in a bun is if she's going to clean the garage.

CHAPTER TWELVE

MY FIRST MURDER CONFESSION

The first time I confessed to murder, I was working for my brother. As I said in an earlier chapter, my brother Joe works in the real estate business. When he started out, he flipped houses. He would buy a shitty property, demolish the inside, and rebuild them to the point he could sell them for a higher price.

My job was demolition. I didn't know how to build things so I did the crap jobs like picking up garbage, painting, or ripping the sheetrock off the walls. One time, I was working by myself at this old place. The house stood on stilts over the water. The kitchen had developed mold and was gutted. During the remodel, my brother asked me to hang new sheetrock and close off an old pantry right off the kitchen.

It didn't take long before I was bored. The wheels of my awful mind started spinning, and I came up with a prank to pass the time. Before I closed off that area I decided I'd leave a note. I got a Sharpie and before I hung the last piece of sheetrock, I wrote a note inside the wall:

Hi, my name is Stewart. I lived here with my grandmother. She was poor and couldn't afford her medications anymore. While I was here, her pain got a lot worse. I hated seeing her like that, so I killed her. I wanted her to be at peace! I didn't have money for a funeral so I buried her under the house. If you are reading this note, please give her a proper burial! You will find her grave marked by a cross of two sticks. I hope whoever finds this understands that I tried to do the right thing.

I signed it with Stewart's name and nailed up that last piece of sheetrock. I crawled under the house and stuck a cross made from two sticks into the ground. I finished up and called it a day.

Awhile later, I told my brother all about it. He just shook his head in disgust and told me I had problems. The whole joke seemed to fall flat and after that, I forgot about it. My twisted little prank sat behind that wall like a hidden bomb. It took a long time before someone lit the fuse.

Sheetrock C.S.I.

Many years later, I was living in Florida. One afternoon, I got a panicked call from Joe.

"Jim, you have to fly back to New Jersey, right now!" He said. My heart dropped. I was sure someone in our family had died.

"Oh, no! Why? What happened?" I asked.

"Do you remember that prank you pulled? You wrote a crazy story on the pantry's wall about Stewart killing his grandmother. Well, that house sold to a new owner, and they remodeled the kitchen and found your story. The owner called the cops and now they have an investigation team at the house as we speak. They have backhoes on the way and they're going to dig for a fucking body!"

"That was over five years ago! How did they trace it back to you?" I asked.

"Supposedly, they traced the code on the sheetrock. They know the year it was bought. Then, they looked up the records and saw I owned the house at the time."

Joe went on to tell me that officers showed up at my parent's house asking for him. My mother was the one that answered the door and asked what it was about. They told her it was regarding a murder investigation at one of Joe's old investment properties. Needless to say, my mother started freaking out thinking her son must have killed someone.

"Mom told them I didn't live there anymore but then the cops threatened her with obstruction of justice if she didn't turn over my new address. She was in tears, Jim!" He said. "But, I had no idea what was going on until they showed up at my house!"

The police officers surprised Joe that same day. It was Saturday morning and he was home with his two little kids.

"I answered the door and they had that fucking piece of sheetrock with them. They showed me your note and wanted to know what I knew about it."

Joe said he laughed and told them one of his construction workers was responsible for the sick prank. "Sorry, officers! That was five years ago. I can't remember who was working for me then but I'm a hundred percent sure it was a joke!"

I laughed as Joe replayed the story for me. Then, his tone changed.

"Look, that's what happened but I left out one thing. They kept pressing me for a name. They wouldn't leave until I gave them one. I'm sorry but I told them it was you."

I freaked out, "WHY WOULD YOU GIVE THEM MY NAME?"

"They were going to charge me, so I had to tell them! They want you to fly home immediately and meet with them."

"YOU MOTHERFUCKER!" I yelled. I hung up on Joe mad as hell. I was completely freaked out and didn't know what to do.

A few minutes later, Joe called me back.

"I'm just fucking with you!" He said.

He was laughing hysterically while I stood there with my mouth hanging open in shock. *Holy Shit! Joe pranked me!* The only false part of the story was him giving them my name. I was mad he turned the tables on me but I was also relieved that I wasn't on my way to prison!

"I GOT YOU, MOTHERFUCKER!" Joe was so damn proud of himself.

KETCHUP IS FOR KIDS

Recently, I read about a restaurant in Florida that banned ketchup for anyone over the age of ten years old. I LOVE THAT!

Ketchup is for kids, not for adults! I know you're a creature of habit and you've been putting ketchup on your food for years. GET OVER IT! It's for kids.

If I get a fresh hamburger off the grill, the last thing I want to do is put liquid sugar on it. I actually want to taste it. Ketchup is liquid sugar and a bunch of strange chemicals. That's all it is! There are over fifty teaspoons of sugar in a bottle of ketchup. There's no reason for that!

I went to lunch with my friend the other day. He got his meal and asked me to pass the ketchup.

I said, "If I'm going to pass the ketchup to you, I'm asking for a booster seat. Because that's what you should sit in if you're eating ketchup at forty-two years old."

NO MORE FUCKING KETCHUP!

Awful Relationships: Man Caves

Man caves are one thing that contributes to awful relationships between men and women. Grown men don't need man caves! When you're a teenager, you hate your parents and you need a lot of space, a place to get away from them. The typical teenager might convert a basement or attic into a private place to smoke pot, play video games, or bang his girlfriend. No problem!

Adult married men with a family don't need a special room to play video games or design a fantasy football team while Mumford & Sons plays in the background. A grown man shouldn't be playing *Wii Golf* or *Call of Duty*. I realize you can't play that shit in the living room because your wife doesn't like it, but guess what, nobody else likes it, either!

Any guy who hides from his wife and kids in a little fucking room has serious issues in his marriage. If you want to be alone, get in your car and drive around the fucking neighborhood. Don't hide in your little playroom because your life is miserable!

Mancavolution

Our dads didn't have man caves. They didn't have a special room for watching TV. They used the living room or den. Dads didn't need separate space, you know why? Our dads were not afraid of our moms! Not that they acted like dicks, but they saw no reason to sequester themselves in a little fucking room downstairs. They hung out in places like the garage where they repaired cars and built shit. They didn't need to prove they were men, they were men! They didn't think about it, they just were!

Today's men grew up being pampered by their mothers and some of them haven't outgrown that. Back in the day, Mom didn't like to have a messy house, so she set aside one room for the kids and called it a playroom.

The playroom was filled with toys, Play-Doh, trains, and plastic dinosaurs. You'd go in there and play or color with your crayons. If you marked on the walls, it didn't matter. The playroom was meant to be a place little boys could do anything they wanted. While that was good strategy for a busy mom, it turned many children into mamas' boys.

These mamas' boys didn't learn how to share living space with other people. They didn't know what it was like to clean up for themselves, then they went to college and repeated the same cycle. They lived with four other guys and became even worse slobs. When they got out of college, they moved in with their girlfriends and got married.

Because these guys are complete disasters, they can't take care of themselves. They still need a mommy so they marry their moms. They let their wives take over the house but they still want that playroom they had in their childhood. They beg permission to take over the basement or a room downstairs. They give their new playroom a more masculine name and instead of Play-Doh they hang up sports posters!

WHAT A BUNCH OF PUSSIES!

Honey, I'll Be in My Homo Fort

There's a lot of gay stuff that goes on in man caves. It shouldn't be called a man cave. It's a fucking homo-fort. I'm not putting down gay people when I say that. I'm pointing out there is a lot of overcompensating going on when you have a guy who can't stop telling anyone that will listen that he's a man! No, you're not. If you have to prove you're a man by having a man cave you really are a pussy! It's that simple.

When I was younger I built a fort and all the boys in the neighborhood would come over and we would hang out. It was a strict no-girls-allowed club. Even though no girls would've wanted to be in there. We were a bunch of losers playing with our wrestling action figures.

In the same way, these pussies love man caves because it's usually the only place in the house they can completely control. Most man caves have a special chair for the dude, collectible toys, stupid sports memorabilia, and dumb man art. In other words, man caves are disasters just like the men that hang out in them.

Hanging up manly art is meant to be one of the big freedoms a man cave gives a guy. Women control the look of the rest of the house. They get one small room or a basement to decorate. They put up shit like posters with hot women, half-naked and bent-over, holding cold beer. Or, the famous velvet painting *Dogs Playing Poker* because dogs smoking cigars is meant to be hilarious. Except no one has ever laughed at that painting. More people have laughed at a mass shooting.

A guy with a man cave will say, "You know what I'm going to put in my man cave? I'm going to hang up a dartboard because we're guys, and real men like dartboards, we play darts."

Stick that dart in your eye, motherfucker!

"I might even have a dart tournament. Hey, you want to come to my man cave this weekend and play darts?"

No, because I'm afraid you will try to play with my dick while I'm in your man cave.

Easy Chair Idiots

Man caves always have a special chair. The chair serves as a throne and no one else is allowed to sit in it without special permission. It's usually a comfortable recliner with two cup-holders for beer.

One of my friends was bragging about this. "You know what I have right next to my easy chair?"

"A box of tampons?" I said.

"No asshole. I have a KEGERATOR!"

"What the hell is that?" I asked.

"It's a refrigerator with a beer tap on it. You tap a small keg and place it in the refrigerator, and then you just pull the handle on top of the kegerator to refill your beer."

While he's down in his man cave, licking foam off that stupid fucking kegerator, some guy is tapping his wife.

Dicks with Dolls

Man caves are famous for having toys and action figures in them. Toys have no place in a grown man's life. Your mother threw out your stupid toys when you left home. She did that for a reason. Women don't want to see men playing with children's toys unless they have been diagnosed with Asperger's.

Another popular man cave decoration is the sports-themed bobblehead. Man cave guys will line their shelves with them. Why the fuck do adult men have collections of dolls?

Do you know why those fucking bobbles are shaking their heads? They're judging you! They're saying, "You're a fucking grown man with dolls on your shelf. Go put them in your toddler's room where they belong."

Bad Memorabilia

The number-one decoration you find in a man cave is sports memorabilia. That's sad because all sports memorabilia is fucking stupid! For instance, there's no reason to have a little frame with a World Series ticket stub from game three in 1998 when the Yankees played the Braves. NOBODY GIVES A SHIT!

It doesn't matter that you saw Scott Brosius hit a double off the wall. WHO GIVES A FUCK?

I bet Scott Brosius doesn't even give a shit! He probably can't remember it. I can hear a fan asking him about that play.

"Oh really? I did that?" Brosius asks.

"You don't remember that?" The fan says.

"No!"

"How could you not remember that?"

"Because it's been fifteen years and I have a life! You should, too! Get the fuck out of here weirdo!"

I can't believe guys buy shit like Derek Jeter baseballs off eBay. Nothing against Derek Jeter, but he cranked a hundred of those out in twenty minutes to make his house payment. There's nothing special about that ball. That ball doesn't belong on your man cave wall; it belongs shoved up your fucking ass! Get some lube and work it right in there! Now you have a memory worth preserving! When you take it out of your ass it will look like Jeter's biracial skin.

Hanging a bunch of sports memorabilia on your wall is dumb. I have a huge basement but I don't want it cluttered with that kind of crap. I don't need to hang a Willie McCovey poster up to remind me he was my favorite player. I know I like the guy! I watched Dan Marino play for seventeen years. I have those memories with me. I don't need his jersey on the wall in a fucking frame! I like eating hamburgers but there is not a picture of one hanging on my fucking wall.

Fuck You, Rudy!

The movie poster for *Rudy* is another common thing you find on man cave walls.

Why? I have no fucking idea! I guess some men get inspiration from that movie and watch it over and over.

That is one of the most overrated movies of all time. It's about an undersized guy that can't make the team but at the end of the movie, he finally gets in the game and makes a sack. I just summed the movie up in three seconds.

You want inspiration? Put a picture of Michael J. Fox on your man cave wall. He's had Parkinson's for twenty years and never bitched once about it. He still works in entertainment, remains married to his wife, raised his kids, and doesn't fucking complain. That's fucking inspiration!

Put a picture of his wife on your wall, too. She's stayed with him through all the hard times! If I had a wife that was diagnosed with Parkinson's, I would leave her in a heartbeat. I have this collection of very nice china that my grandmother left me. These are expensive antique plates. I couldn't take a chance that she'd shake and drop that shit. I couldn't live the rest of my life using paper plates and cups. However, I'd make sure to get at least one last hand job from her because I'm sure it would be pretty good if she had that disease.

Here's the bottom line about sports memorabilia, if you're a forty-year-old man and you're still putting Dallas Cowboy posters up in your man cave, let it go, motherfucker. You really need to ask yourself why you're excited about looking at a poster of Troy Aikman, Michael Irvin, and Emmitt Smith every fucking day. The 1994 Super Bowl was over twenty fucking years ago. Stop living in the past. NOBODY GIVES A SHIT!

I think these men secretly like looking at Troy Aikman's ass. Maybe that's why they get a chair with two cup-holders. One to hold a beer and the other for tissues and hand cream.

Just shut off all the man cave's power, sit there in the dark, and think about your life. Think about what the fuck went wrong. Why are you stuck in the basement while your wife controls the rest of the house? Put your balls in a nice jar and place it on your man cave mantle. Then, sit back and contemplate how you became such a fucking pussy!

I'd rather hang out with the Taliban in a cave in Afghanistan than be in some guy's man cave. I'd rather have a fucking sharp knife to my neck and a videotape of me yelling shit in fucking Arabic than hang out in a fucking man cave, looking at a Derek Jeter bobblehead, dumb action figures, and a *Rudy* poster while playing *Wii Golf*. I'd rather have my fucking head cut off and held up and shown to my family. That's what I think of your fucking man cave!

Awful Relationships:
Parents Should Be Sprayed

Awful parents become awful when they turn parenting into an obsession. These parents insist that their kids are special or better than all the other kids, but they're not! The majority of children are normal, run-of-the-mill kids. They're not exceptional but awful parents refuse to believe that.

Awful parents force their kids into things they don't want to do. Athletics is a good example. Parents think their kid will be the next football or basketball star and they push them into a crazy training and game schedule. That's so fucking stupid!

If you're one of these parents, stop that shit! Don't force baseball on your kid just because you played baseball. I'm sure if we watched the videotapes of your games, we'd see you weren't any good, either. You like to tell the story differently, but it's all bullshit. You sucked, and if your kid doesn't have a natural aptitude for baseball, he'll suck too. Don't live in the fucking past! Find something your kid's good at naturally!

Focus on what your kid likes. That's all you have to do. Maybe the kid isn't good at sports but he's a nerd and he's good at electronics and shit like that. Maybe he'll be the next Bill Gates. That's a fucking good gig!

He can't swing a fucking bat. He couldn't kick a soccer ball. He didn't know how to throw a football. All right, this kid is fucking awful at sports. So what? He may be a computer whiz and create some great technology to get rid of awful parents! That would make him one of the greatest inventors in history!

I remember hitting home runs when I was in Little League. Whoop-dee-fucking-doo! Who gives a shit? I wasn't that great but in my little town I stood out and was considered a great player.

As soon as I got on the freshmen high school team, I was benched after two games. In that group of players, I wasn't good enough to keep going. I wasn't mad at the coach. I didn't have my mom go sit down with the athletic director and argue to get me back on the field. My dad didn't make a big stink. He saw I was batting eighth, and the pitcher was throwing faster than I could handle. Even he said, "All right, holy shit! You're not going far with this baseball career!"

No one freaked out. It was understood that I would do something else.

That's not how it is now. Recently, I was at my son's T-ball game on a Saturday morning. I only signed him up because he's really good at it. I don't like going to these games because you have to listen to parents talk about stupid shit like problems in the school districts. I'd rather suck my friend off in his man cave after a round of darts.

Anyway, when a kid hit the ball, these parents were fucking screaming like the team had just won the World Series. There were fucking seventeen errors on the play. The kid didn't hit a home run. He just kept running. He didn't even know to stop. He missed two bases along the way too. If that were televised it would be on the greatest sports blooper of all time.

The kid's parents were yelling, "Aiden made a home run! Yeah, Aiden!"

Made a home run? Aiden didn't make a home run. He hit a weak ground ball to second! I wish that fucking kid would've tripped and fallen on his face. Of course, his parents would sue whoever put the second base bag down. Good parenting, you fucks!

Later in my life, I decided I wanted to be a singer so I signed up for lessons.

During my first lesson, the teacher said, "Look, I could sit here and take your money every week for the next two years, but you really don't have an ear for music. Sorry, kid, you don't have what it takes. You stink!"

I could have thrown a fit and said, fuck you, teacher! But, I knew that even though I loved music, Lou Ferrigno had a better ear for music than me.

Finally, I realized I liked comedy, and that's what I pursued as my career.

I also knew it wasn't going to be easy. If I thought my parents would swoop in and make things right, I would have never pushed myself.

When I started doing comedy in New York City, I auditioned and the bookers told me I was terrible. They said I couldn't work at their clubs. When that happened, I didn't go home and cry. I didn't write the fucking comedy club a letter. I went home and wrote better jokes until they were forced to use me because I was doing well onstage.

The bottom line is if your kids suck at something, don't threaten to file a lawsuit. Move the fuck on and find something else your kid is good at. If you have your son taking karate at five don't expect him to make a living at it later in life. What is the reason to take karate as a kid anyway? I'm not sure, other than to help fend off the local priest. Then again, a priest might get off on getting a karate chop to the sack.

Awful Relationships: Baby Names

Giving children stupid fucking names is another way awful parents fuck up their children. These parents shouldn't be allowed to name their own children. Hospitals should have a special committee that picks a random name from a list of super-fucking normal names. That would ensure kids don't have to deal with being teased and picked on their entire lives.

Baby, That's a Fucking Bad Name!

When my ex-wife was pregnant, she bought a baby name book like every other woman. I guess it's a fucking tradition for pregnant women, but I didn't need a book to name my kid. The book was the size of *War and Peace*. She went through it for six weeks looking over every single name. I went through it in seconds and picked out three possible names: Larry, Luke, and Lenny.

My choices were run-of-the-mill names. Awful parents pick crazy names because they think their kid is special, but they're really not.

"He kicked a lot when he was in my womb!" They say. But, all babies kick. There is nothing special about that.

"We knew he would be special, we had a special feeling about him! That's why we named him Bennett!"

That special feeling you had was the feeling of being fat, bloated, and constipated. Bennett had nothing to do with that shit. However, if Bennett pops out of your snatch and starts doing my taxes, I'll tell everyone he's the greatest kid ever born!

Out of the three names, we picked Luke. You can't mock a normal name like that. I didn't spell it L-u-u-k-e, either! You don't need to give the other children extra ammo to use against you. If you don't believe me, name your kid Cooper. Wait until the teacher calls out his name in class and everyone snickers. Your kid will come home and complain to you, and all you'll be able to say is, "It's okay, Coop!"

Cooper is popular because it's a trendy Irish name. Parents should stay away from those names, too, because they are beyond brutal! No kid should ever be named Decklyn, Aiden, or Liam. If you name your kid Decklyn, you've committed child abuse! I'd rather name my kid Little Dick. Little Dick Florentine sounds much better than Decklyn Florentine.

Why Katniss Killed Her Parents

The trend over the last decade is to name your kid after a character in a movie. Katniss from the *Hunger Games* has become a popular name. I don't know anyone that saw *Hunger Games* so I can't tell you a fucking thing about Katniss! I don't even know what that movie was about. I guess someone is chased in the movie. Wow, how fucking original and how fucking terrible if you name your daughter Katniss. It sounds like "cat piss" and that's exactly what the kids will call her for the rest of her life!

The abuse she will take as a kid with that nickname will push her into the world of stripping. At least in that job, she'll change her name to Porsche so she won't have to deal with being called Katniss.

The *Twilight* movies were another terrible flash-in-the-pan. Do awful parents really think *Twilight* will be a classic like *The Godfather*? Imagine twenty years from now, when someone is asking Jasper, Cullen, or Bella, where their name came from and they have to explain it's from some shit movie that teenagers watched and forgot about a week later. I wouldn't call one of my turds Jasper! I'd rather call my daughter Cunt then Cullen.

Shitty Spellings

I read about a kid named ABCDE. My only response to that was Y?

But, there is something worse, parents that change the spelling of normal names trying to be clever.

One time, I heard a parent bragging about this. "We're going to name our son Michael but spell it M-y-k-u-l because he's going to be special so he needs a unique name!"

He's not unique, he's cursed! Cursed with stupid fucking parents!

Mykul will grow up with a ton of resentment! Every time Mykul has to spell his name that repressed rage will grow a bit more!

"How do you spell your name, kid?"

"M-y-k-u-l."

"Wow, I've never heard Michael spelled that way before."

"Yeah, well for the millionth time, my parents thought that was a good way to spell it!"

"Are your parents illiterate, son? Didn't they double-check the spelling on the birth certificate before they left the hospital?"

"Oh no, they knew what they were doing. My parents are just FUCKING DOUCHEBAGS!"

CHAPTER THIRTEEN

THAT METAL SHOW

I grew up listening to heavy metal. My two older brothers Bob and Joe got me into the music. I'd be in the backseat of the car and they would be cranking Black Sabbath, AC/DC, Ted Nugent, and more. I became obsessed with that music and read every liner note on every album I bought. I didn't do well in school but I can reel off every birthday of all the members of Black Sabbath. Little did I know years later I would co-hosting a show on TV called *That Metal Show*. The show ran from 2008 to 2015. We interviewed hard rock and metal bands from the 80s. It was basically *The Tonight Show* for AC/DC fans. After I got divorced in 2014, I was hoping that maybe I could meet some women because I was on a TV show. The problem was our demographic was forty-year-old males and the show aired on Saturday nights. There weren't a lot of hot chicks staying in on a Sat night because we were interviewing the bass player from Ratt. Basically if I wanted to fuck forty-year-old guys that wear Rush concert T-shirts I would be in sex rehab.

CONCERTS: PEOPLE THAT BLOCK YOUR VIEW

I went to a concert the other night and couldn't see a damn thing because so many things were blocking my view.

I had six guys in front of me and five of them were filming the concert on their smartphones. The sixth guy was using a fucking flip phone to do the same thing. What in the fuck is that guy thinking? Where can you upload video from a flip phone?

They made a point of filming the most popular songs. What are you going to do with that footage? Put it on fucking YouTube? If you go to YouTube and look up that band's most popular songs, you'll see that there are 150 better versions of that song, professionally shot and recorded with six special cameras. The video you have on your cell phone is complete garbage by comparison. It stinks and there's not one damn person interested in seeing it!

But, that won't stop you from taking it to work on Monday!

"Hey, do you want to see the footage I shot of Journey playing "Don't Stop Believin'" at the concert?"

"NO! Unless . . . the singer shit his pants when he was trying to hit a high note?"

"No, it's just the song."

"Then, NO, I don't want to see it. I wasn't there I DON'T CARE! And besides I just heard that song three times on my car ride to work today! That's the last fucking song I want to hear!"

Are you going to bring that to your job at the construction site and play it for your coworkers? You have five hung-over guys busy doing a hard job and they don't give a shit. There's a circle saw buzzing, guys hammering nails on the roof, pickup trucks dumping stuff, jackhammers going off, and you're trying to play that shit video on a speakerphone! Oh yeah, that's going to sound great!

Another thing blocking my view at the concert was the guy on the front row holding up a homemade sign with the band's name on it. What a fucking idiot! We know you're a fan, dude. We're all fans; we're all at the same show! You're in the third row, you paid $300 for that fucking ticket. I have a feeling you're a fan. You don't have to announce it to the world!

And, why did you put the name of the band on your shitty sign? Do you think a band like Iron Maiden is confused about the songs they should sing? Do you think those signs remind them what to play?

"Hey look at that sign! Oh shit, why are we playing a Journey song, we're Iron Maiden. Thank God for that dumb sign! Come on guys, let's play 'Number of the Beast'!"

Here's another thing, it seems like whenever I go to a concert the guy with the biggest head is standing in front of me. I hate that shit. It ruins your night.

Instead of handing out seats based on price, we should measure everyone's head when they enter the venue. The people with the biggest heads have to stand in the back against the wall so they don't block the view!

Next time you go to a concert put your cell phones down, put your fucking signs down, and move your big-ass pumpkin heads—I WANT TO WATCH THE SHOW!

Awful People You Meet: Awful Drivers

My career choice hasn't protected me from the bad part of living a life on the road—horrible fucking drivers! They are everywhere! Get out on any road in America, you'll find them there, some of the most awful people in the fucking world!

Bad drivers are all over the place, and it's worse because they don't realize how much they fucking stink! Most of them are oblivious! When you are behind the wheel, pay attention to what you're doing and where you're going.

FOCUS, MOTHERFUCKERS!

Better Bad Drivers

It's strange how we make everything a competition in America. It doesn't matter what town I'm in, I hear the same thing.

"Oh, the drivers suck around here. You had better watch out if you drive in this town! We definitely have the worst drivers in the country!"

I've never heard people say, "Oh man, and wait until you get out on the road. We have the BEST DRIVERS in the nation!"

It's the same thing when people talk about law enforcement.

"Be careful, the cops suck around here!"

No one has anything encouraging to say. Can you imagine if they did?

"Don't worry about getting pulled over around here, the cops are awesome!"

I'd love to be that driver!

"Man, the other night, I was driving down the road, drinking a beer, smoking weed, and when I was waiting at a stoplight a super nice cop drove up next to me. He rolled his window down and said, 'Hey, dude! Is that good weed? It is? Great! Just remember, it's better to do that at home. Okay, buddy have a great night and drive home safe and don't spill that beer!'"

Now, that would be a fucking cool cop! But, no one has told me a story like that. I wonder why?

Could it be that cops are stopping people because they're doing stupid shit like drinking and driving? All cops don't suck. Your town doesn't have worse cops than the next town over. The problem is you don't interact with police officers unless you're doing something wrong! For instance, my friend got a ticket for doing 75 mph in a 25 mph zone. He couldn't stop complaining.

"Fucking cops suck around here! I got four points because of that ticket! Bastards!"

I know that's so unfair that you were only doing 50 mph over the speed limit. The cops really are assholes around here.

THE REAL ASSHOLE IS YOU!

Exit Here, Idiot!

My biggest pet peeve while driving is when someone misses their exit on the highway and backs up on the shoulder to correct their mistake. Don't fucking do that! That's the dumbest thing you could do!

Just go to the next exit and turn around. That's five extra minutes out of your life. Backing up on the highway is so fucking dangerous and every car going by slows down to see what you're doing and now every nosy fuck wants to know what they're missing.

Whenever I see that, I wish I were a cop. I'd pull you over and plant cocaine in your trunk.

I swear if I see someone doing that again, I will pull over and park right behind that person and take my cell phone out, and pretend I have an emergency call. Anything to prevent an asshole like that from pulling that dick move!

Double-Parked Douchebag

I hate when people double-park their car. It's especially horrendous when it happens in New York City.

Hey douchebag, you're blocking a lane when you do that! Drop your dumb girlfriend off in front of the stupid store and circle the block until she comes out.

Or, if there is an empty spot, even if it is illegal, pull in there, and wait. As long as you stay in the car, you can move if it becomes a problem. Pull in front of a fucking fire hydrant, who gives a shit. Your dumb wife will be back in five minutes.

By the way, using your hazard lights doesn't excuse double-parking. That's not fooling anyone!

"Oh, I guess I overreacted. He has his hazards on. It must be an emergency!"

Believe me, no one is thinking that. They're calling you every horrible and disgusting name in the book, and topping that off with a few choice racial slurs.

Move your fucking car, douchebag!

Stomp Their Rubber Necks!

Rubbernecking is another one that annoys the shit out of me. If you drive a car you've been in traffic jams caused by people slowing down to gawk at accidents. If you're guilty of this shit, STOP IT!

It's so fucking frustrating when a simple drive home takes four fucking hours because some dumb bitch slows down to see the aftermath of a wreck.

"Wow! What's going on?"

"Oh look at that, that's a serious fender bender!"

"Sure is! Damn, that's a nice car too. Sucks for him!"

If someone died it'll be on the local news when you get home. You won't miss it so keep going! You really don't need to look, it's not that interesting. Just mind your own fucking business and look straight ahead.

Whenever I roll up on an accident and cars are slowing down to look, I lay on my horn as hard as fucking possible.

BEEEEEEEEEPPPPPPPPPPPP!

I hold it down like it's fucking broken. I won't stop until they turn around and look at me with a dumb expression plastered on their face!

"Whoa! What are you beeping for dude?"

"JUST GO MOTHERFUCKER! GO STRAIGHT, GO!"

I'm so brutal about this that the victim on the stretcher they pulled out of the wreck looks over at me!

"What's the rush dude? They're still looking for my leg!"

Let's Watch the Shame Film!

I have the solution to all this bad driving. I want to film every car driving down the road for a month straight. Film all their bad habits, how fast they drive, how they change lanes, and all the minor things like using turn signals. Then, I want to sit everyone in a room and show them the video footage, and go over every bad move they made.

"What the fuck were you thinking here? There was a car right next to you and you tried to change lanes without checking. You could have caused an accident! Why did you slow down here? What the fuck were you looking at? Mind your own damn business when you're on the highways! Look at this clip, asshole! Why were you leaving so much space between you and the car in front of you? Move over to the slow lane if you're going to do this shit!"

It will be like a football player having to watch the game film with a coach after losing a big game.

"Do you remember making this stupid fucking move? Don't drive like that, or we're taking your car away from you!"

All these bad drivers need to endure the humiliation of watching their fuck-ups, over and over again like the football player cleaning up his mistakes. I'm admittedly an aggressive driver. When someone gets nervous in my car I just tell them the same thing. "Do you see any dents on my car? No! Then, go back to staring into your phone and shut your fucking hole!"

The Color of Road Rage

Now, let's discuss the worst drivers by ethnicity. First, I know it's a cliché to say the Asian drivers are bad, but they are fucking terrible!

I'll skip that group because to me the absolute worst driver is the white male.

If you see someone driving like a complete asshole, weaving in and out of traffic, not using the blinker, speeding, or slowing down to flip people off because they have road rage—it's a white dude! It's undeniable, the white male is an aggressive and angry driver.

I think you can trace all this stupid rage back to a white man's home life. He is angry because he's not in a happy relationship. His wife is a cunt, his kids hate him, and he doesn't like his job. He only took his shit job because he had to support his family. So, he goes through life pissed off because he's locked in a prison of misery. When he leaves the house he brings that anger and rage with him and drives like an asshole. In my book, these guys are the most dangerous drivers because they're ticking time bombs. He can't tell his fucking wife she's a twat so he takes it out on the road.

Whitey at the Wheel

White females are bad drivers, too. They are constantly distracted. They text, talk on the phone, babble about unimportant bullshit, fix their hair in the rearview mirror, or put on makeup. They're constantly fiddling with the fucking radio because they can't go one second without hearing a pop song.

On the flip side, you have the fat soccer mom in the minivan that's overly cautious. In many ways, she's worse. She has her two hands nervously vise-gripped to the steering wheel at all times. She will only do about 50 mph on the highway but stays in the fast lane and is too scared to move over. You can't talk sense into this dumb bitch because she has the ultimate defense.

"Sorry, I'm not speeding. I have my kids in the back. I'm not going to do 75 miles per hour just because you're in a rush. If you don't like it, too bad!"

I've given up fucking with these women. Take it from me, just drive around these bitches, and let it go. Count your blessings she's not black!

Stay Off the Road, Shaniqua!

Black guys aren't that bad on the road. I guess they can't be—it gives cops another reason to pull them over. But, black men have one driving quirk that makes me fucking crazy. They ride the brake while they're driving at high speeds. That's why they constantly get pulled over. They ride the brake so much they always have a taillight out.

Driving like that messes up the flow of traffic because once the driver flashes the brake every other asshole on the road will brake too. But, this is nothing compared to the problems a black woman causes on the road.

The black female is the worst driver on the road. She is oblivious to what's going on and doesn't give a fuck! If they're in a fast lane, they're doing 45 mph, and don't care if people are honking at them, or flashing their lights, signaling to move over. A black woman doesn't care, she won't move for anyone, she doesn't give a shit if people are screaming, or giving her the fucking finger. She's in her own little world, driving slow as shit, and fucking up the fast lane for everyone else.

If you piss off a black female, you might get some honking, yelling, or she'll rip her weave off and throw it at you. She may flip you off or cuss you out. But, don't look at her, just stare straight ahead with an attitude that says, *whatever bitch*; you're not my fucking problem! Maybe she'll understand what you are really saying:
STAY OFF THE FUCKING ROAD, SHANIQUA!

The Left Turn Trick

I have a good trick for faking out awful drivers when I'm at a traffic light and need to make a left turn. I've noticed if I'm the first car waiting, and I have my left turn signal blinking, the asshole coming my way will always gun the engine to make sure I don't turn in front of him. I don't understand why people do that but they do it every time!

So, if I need to turn, I wait without my signal. The second the light turns green, I hit the left blinker, and quickly turn left in front of that stupid motherfucker. It works every time because that asshole is surprised, and I have the jump on him. He can honk at me all he wants afterwards. I got shit to do and places to go.

Stopping at Yield Signs

Awful drivers don't know how to use yield signs properly. They're the ones that come to a complete stop when you approach a yield sign.

Hey asshole, you need momentum to get on the highway. You've had your own lane for half a mile. When you see the yield sign two hundred yards away, watch the traffic and use some fucking common sense to anticipate how to merge. Yield doesn't mean come to a complete stop! It means proceed with caution, dickhead!

Green Light Breakers

Another awful driver is the asshole that hits his brake when the light is green! Why are you fucking hitting the brake when you have the right of way? No one is in front of you? Traffic is flowing and you want to slow down, why? I understand if you want to be cautious because it's yellow. But, why are you riding the brakes when it's fucking green! *Come on, motherfucker! You're not even a black guy!*

Parking Space Fake-Out

Have you noticed how awful drivers insist on parking next to the entrance of a store or mall? You can see there are a hundred other spaces to choose from but these idiots sit next to the first two spots, hazard lights flashing, engines idling, waiting for the people who own those cars to come out of the store. They'll wait forever. It's so fucking stupid!

Women are especially bad at this. They get aggravated when you park away from the entrance.

"Can't you find anything closer to the door?"

"What does it matter?" I always say. "Were you expecting me to give you a piggyback ride while we're in there? You'll probably do twenty miles while you walk around the mall. Why does it matter if we park in the back lot and walk a few extra feet?"

I like to fuck with people that need to park up close. I like to do this in a mall parking lot, especially around the holidays, when it's packed with shoppers. I leave the mall with a lot of packages and walk to the closest car. I'll stand there fumbling for my keys for an obnoxiously long time, pretending the car is mine.

These lazy-ass people hover nearby hoping to get my space. It's easy to imagine what they are thinking, it's written all over their faces.

"Oh, great! This guy has the best spot, and he's leaving. It's my lucky day!"

So, while they wait patiently, I fuck with them. I don't make eye contact. Instead, I stall as long as I can. I go through my pockets or pretend to talk on my phone. If they yell out and ask me questions, I won't answer. If they persist, I'll start an argument.

"Are you leaving?"

"No! Why?"

"Well, I see that you're standing by your car looking for your keys."

"Yeah, so what? Are you saying I can't stand by my car?"

"No, I was just hoping I could take your spot since it's so close."

That's when I hit them with something like this:

"Judging by the three chins you have, you should park in the back, and burn a few calories!"

Awful People You Meet: Awful Navigators

I am not a fan of the GPS or the navigation systems that are installed in cars. The apps on our smartphones like *Waze* work way better. The factory-installed ones cause too much unnecessary tension in people's lives. And, they've turned normally smart people into awful fucking navigators.

On the way to a party recently, one of my friends called me and bragged that he would be there early because he was using his GPS system in his new truck. That same guy ended up being three hours late! The party started at 8 p.m. and they finally showed up at 11 p.m. The rest of his passengers were pissed. The entire trip took over four fucking hours!

Once his friends got out of the car and joined the party, they refused to talk to him. That included his wife. While they were coming in, half of the people were leaving because it was time for most people to turn around and go home. This guy was making excuses all night.

"I punched the address in my GPS and it sent me to the Pennsylvania Turnpike instead of the NJ Turnpike."

"Didn't you think you were going the wrong way when you saw signs for Pittsburgh?"

"Yeah, but I trusted that the GPS would know where we were going!"

Yeah, too bad it didn't send you off a fucking cliff!

Whenever, I rent a car they ask me if I want a GPS unit for an extra $9.99 per day. Who the fuck would pay for that? I said to the guy behind the desk, "I would take it if I still had a beeper."

Navigating the Dark Ages

Do you ever wonder how our parents lived without GPS? How did they leave the fucking house? When their friends invited them over for a barbecue, did they turn down the invitation?

"We'd love to come, it sounds so fun, but we have no idea how to get there. Thanks anyway!"

Seriously, were the roads completely empty before the GPS? How did truck drivers make their fucking deliveries?

I'll watch old football games from the 70s on the NFL network with 70,000 fans packed in the stadium. I can't even focus on the game. All I think about is how the fuck did they find the stadium without a GPS?

Old Maps

The only good thing about the GPS is that it replaced the paper map! Do you remember those from your childhood?

You're a kid driving around with your father and he gets lost and asks you to open up the map and figure out the route. You unfold it and the map takes up three quarters of the fucking front seat. Now, your father can barely see because it's covering most of the windshield. So, your Dad has to roll down the window, so he can see well enough to drive. He looks like Jim Carrey in *Ace Ventura* leaning out the fucking window driving with a busted windshield.

You finally get Dad back on course and he orders you to fold up the map.

"Fold that up—EXACTLY LIKE IT WAS BEFORE—and then put it back in the glove box!"

Now you spend the rest of the car ride trying to fold it back together in the correct way. Solving a Rubik's Cube is easier than folding this fucking map back together. Dad puts pressure on you to fold it right. You get nervous and sweat. Your dad looks over and he's not paying attention to the road. He slams on his brakes because he's so obsessed with making you fold the map correctly. He wants to pull over and fold the map himself. You remind him that your destination is still eighteen hours away and you still have time to figure it out. But he doesn't care so he pulls over to the shoulder. That's when you explode on him.

"Fucking, relax! Do you really need to pull over to fold this map so it can fit in the fucking glove compartment? Next gas station we stop at I'll buy you a new map for $1.49 you cheap obsessive-compulsive fuck!"

CHAPTER FOURTEEN

ACTING AWFUL

These days there is a lot of talk about how hard it is to make a living. Most people I grew up with made smart choices about their lives and careers and took on stable jobs. They enrolled in health insurance and set up 401ks. I didn't grow up until I was forty. I was crazy enough to pursue my dreams. Which is a good thing because if I had ended up in a cubicle like in *Office Space*, I would have murdered my coworkers during a Hawaiian shirt Friday and gone to prison.

Coming Full Circle

I started doing stand-up comedy because I wanted to be onstage somehow and I failed miserably trying to be a musician. Then I took acting classes to learn that craft and also to make out with hot chicks in class. I'd always pick scenes to do where there was some heavy making out. The best part about that was rehearsing the scene over and over again at my apartment. I was having so much fun I didn't even need a girlfriend!

Cut to years later and I get a role in Amy Schumer's *Trainwreck* and in *Californication* and got submitted for an Emmy for best guest star in an episode of the TV series *Louie*. I should have got an Emmy for my role in a movie with Jenna Fischer called *A Little Help*. I had to dry hump her in a scene. All that practice in my apartment from acting class had me nail that scene in one take. I'm lucky it was only one take. If we did another one I would have blown a load in my pants. I'm premature Pete.

SHITTY CELL PHONES

I got a new smartphone two weeks ago. Fully charged, the battery on that piece of shit lasts about an hour and ten minutes.

I've been writing this section of the book for thirty seconds. Now, the charge on the phone is down to 47 percent.

Everywhere I go, I have to take my charger with me. When I walk into a room I look no one in the eye, I look for an empty outlet. If I see an outlet, it's like seeing a naked woman. I get a fucking erection! I want to stick my dick in that outlet! And, it would fit, too. I have no girth—unless I have a bad case of warts!

I'm a simple man and I don't need this awful fucking technology. If the next upgrade doesn't work any better, I'm going back to the old flip phone. Remember that first flip phone you got twenty years ago? My uncle still has that phone. It has been sitting on his table for eight months, turned on, and it's still charged at 59 percent.

When he tries to take a picture with that phone, it comes out like a Polaroid. I want that smartphone!

I know if I turn my phone off it will obviously save the battery life. The problem is you can't turn your fucking phone off; otherwise, people think you are dead, kidnapped, or cheating! That's how fucked-up things have become!

"My call went straight to voicemail, I checked Google Earth looking to see if I saw an accident on your path home. I was so worried!"

Jesus! Fucking relax! This is why everyone in this country is on Xanax—these fucking awful phones!

Awful Traditions: Superstitions

Awful people are fucking stupid and they try to spread that stupidity to the rest of us. One way they do that is by imposing their awful superstitions on everyone around them.

Worrying about good luck is fucking stupid. Whatever happens will happen. Don't blame it on black cats, open umbrellas, spilled salt, or other stupid shit like that.

If you really think about it, you cause most of the bad luck in your life. You make bad decisions. You do dumb things. People say you create your own luck, well that applies to bad luck, too.

"I've got such bad luck when it comes to relationships!"

"No, you don't. You're just picking the wrong person because you like mothering men who are walking disasters. That's what your mom did; now you do it."

You always being in bad relationships has everything to do with you and nothing to do with that open ladder you walked under last week.

Knock on Wood

Superstitious people live life like it's a fucking fairy tale!

"I've got a great job. What can I tell you? I'm lucky, knock on wood."

"Wait a minute, are you telling me you think you have good luck because you knocked on a piece of wood? Are you fucking brain dead?"

There's no arguing with people like this.

"So, you think a piece of magical wood is keeping your whole life together. You don't think it might have something to do with the company that hired you? That company makes millions of dollars and has been going strong for years and years. They make shit people buy and have customers all over the world. Don't you think that might be the reason they had an opening at your location? Isn't that the reason you were hired to help the company grow? No? You think it's because you tapped your knuckles on a piece of wood?"

One time, one of my superstitious friends called me in the middle of the night. It was 3 a.m. and he sounded really upset.

"Dude, can you come pick me up? My car broke down. I'm stranded on the side of the road!"

"Oh, wow! Okay, yeah, I can do that. What happened?" I asked.

"It's weird, man. I was at this party and I was telling someone that my Honda Accord has 250,000 miles on it. I bragged it has never broken down. But, shit! I was buzzed and I forgot to knock on wood after I said that! Now, look what's happened."

After hearing his explanation, I was completely silent!

"Hello? Are you still there?" he asked.

"Yeah, I'm here. Let me get this right, you think the reason your Honda Accord is on the side of the road is that you forgot to knock on wood? You don't think it has something to do with the 250,000 miles on your car? The wear and tear had nothing to do with you breaking down?"

"Man, it was working fine before tonight. It broke down because I bragged and then didn't knock on wood!"

I couldn't believe what I was hearing! So, I asked him one more time. "Look dude, we've been friends a long time. You really think you're on the side of road at three o'clock in the morning because you didn't knock on wood?"

"Yeah man, without a doubt," he said.

"Let me ask you one more thing. I know you're hoping I'll come pick your ass up in the middle of the night, but did you knock on wood before you called me?"

"No! I didn't think I needed to do that," he said.

"Well, go find a tree motherfucker!"

CLICK!

I never talked to him again.

No-Hitters

Another place you find awful superstitions is the sports world. Baseball is one of the worst offenders. You could write a set of encyclopedias about all the stupid baseball superstitions.

Take a no-hitter game, for instance. A pitcher who pitches a no-hitter for six or seven innings is considered blessed with luck. The superstition dictates that all the other players on the pitcher's team have to leave him alone while he's in the dugout. The pitcher has to sit in the fucking corner alone. No one can say a word to him. If you do, you break the good luck spell and jinx him.

I can't believe grown men believe this shit, especially in a game known for its love of statistics. If you look at the evidence, you'll find this superstition is total bullshit. Out of 100 pitchers who pitched a no-hitter through six innings, 97 fail to get the remaining nine outs they need. In other words, only 3 percent of pitchers, in this unique situation, pitch a no-hitter. Yet, these grown-ass men treat the pitcher like he has some horrible disease when he returns to the dugout.

If I were on that team I'd go right over to the pitcher and get as close as possible and I'd have a speech ready for the occasion.

"Dude, you've got nine outs to go. You're a free agent at the end of the year. If you throw this no-hitter you will get at least an extra $10 million in a new contract. Somebody's going to overpay you because of this game. If you get the next nine outs in a row, I'm bringing two hookers to your room tonight. Is that motivation enough for you to go out there and kick some fucking ass?"

That's what should be going on in that dugout.

At the press conference, I imagine he'd thank me.

The press would ask, "How did you win this one? It was obvious you were incredibly focused on those last three innings. Your fastball went from 92 miles per hour to 96 miles per hour and you mowed those guys down. Where did you get that extra gas in your tank?"

"I have to give credit where credit is due. Florentine came over and said he would buy me two hookers tonight if I threw a no-hitter! I've never had a threesome before so I reached back those last three innings and came through!"

The Beards

Beards in baseball—that's another superstition we should ban! Most men don't look good with beards, but baseball players think it's cool to grow them during the playoffs. They look like a bunch of wannabe hipsters out on the field. They might as well wear skinny jeans when they come up to the plate.

"Let's grow beards. The whole team should do it! The rule is we can't shave until the playoffs are over. It'll show team unity."

Seriously? Is that the best idea you have to show team unity? By the way why in the hell are you waiting until the end of the season to show team unity?

You just played 162 games. It's a seven-month season. You started in the fucking middle of February with spring training and played all the way to October with only three weeks off. You played baseball for seven months and now suddenly, during the last two weeks of the season, you have the bright idea to focus on team unity?

Maybe you've had too much fucking unity. You fly in the same plane. You take the same bus to the games. You practice together. You even shower together. Maybe you're getting your periods together because this is a shitty idea!

Show me the stats for a player growing a beard for the playoffs. Then, show me the stats for the two weeks before growing the beard. I want to see his batting average. If he batted .310 the last two weeks of the season and with his beard he's batting .190, I suggest to you "playoff beards" are a fucking fairy tale!

Usually, both teams grow beards and one of them has to lose so all of this makes no fucking sense. When my team is in the playoffs, and they're growing beards, I never think my team has the advantage. I just think after the game my team is going to drink PBRs and listen to music on vinyl.

Rally Caps

What about the "rally caps" superstition? That's another thing we should ban from sports! Have you seen this at games? Oh, it's so fucking fun!

If the team is down by a few runs, fans turn their baseball caps inside out, flip up the lids, and put them on backwards. *Isn't that fucking special?* Who is the genius that came up with this superstition? I'd like to thank him by taking a shit in his rally cap!

Fans really get into this bullshit. If it worked don't you think the organization would make announcements about it and encourage the fans to bring their caps to every game? You know why they don't do that? Because that's retarded.

My six-year-old son is starting to play baseball. Why should I lie to him about these pathetic superstitions? He's young and susceptible to believing just about anything. If I teach him rally caps work and his team loses, he will go home bummed out. One day he'll confront me about my stupid lie.

"Hey Dad, how come the team didn't win? We put the hats on backwards!"

"Son, that doesn't work. It's a superstition people think is fun."

"So, you lied to me?" He asks.

"Yes, like I lied to you about Santa, the Easter Bunny, and the Tooth Fairy. You really think I would let a stranger called the Tooth Fairy come in your room in the middle of the night? The only way he wouldn't molest you is if you had a rally cap on, felt bad, and thought you were retarded for wearing your hat that way."

Bird Shit

Some people have a superstition about bird shit. They think it's good luck when a bird shits in your hair!

NO, THAT'S BAD LUCK!

Any time you have shit in your hair that's a bad day!

Why would anyone think that? Did you ever watch the news and see some assholes talking about how bird shit helped them win the lottery?

"Oh, you won't believe this. I never played the lottery before but I was walking on the beach and a seagull shit in my hair! I said to myself, this is my lucky day, and I walked down to the 7-11 and bought a Powerball ticket and won $300 million dollars!"

Never happened. If a bird shit in my hair and later that day I had a one-night stand with Scarlett Johansson I still wouldn't consider that good luck from the bird turd. I would think, *I can't believe she walked away from her drink long enough for me to Bill Cosby her.*

Umbrellas

"If you open an umbrella inside, that's bad luck."

Have you heard this superstition? I never understood this one. So, I researched it and read the umbrella has feelings and gets pissed off if you don't use it properly. I remember talking about it on stage one night and a woman in the audience yelled out.

"Yeah, I never open them inside!"

"Why?" I asked. "What happens if you open your umbrella inside your house?"

"I don't know," she said.

"Seriously, what do you think might happen if you do?"

"The walls fall down!"

I swear to God that is what she said!

Imagine that scene. You run over to the house and see the coroner taking a woman out in a body bag. Police tape is everywhere because the fucking house fell in on itself. The local cops are standing around scratching their heads. Everything is destroyed like a bomb went off. Then, the press arrives and asks questions.

"Officer, can you give us an update on what happened? Was it a bomb? Was it a gas leak? What happened?"

"Well, we're not entirely sure yet. What we know so far is that the owner opened her umbrella inside the house. The next thing she knew the walls collapsed and the house imploded."

One time, my friend Joe Howard and I went to a local Walmart and grabbed a pair of umbrellas, opened them, and walked up and down the aisles like it was raining. We just wanted to annoy the shit out of people. I'll never forget how this woman with a basket full of clothes got pissed off and yelled at me.

"Sir, you're going to give me bad luck with that open umbrella!"

I said, "Miss, you shop for your clothes at Walmart. Your life was shit before I opened this umbrella, don't blame me!"

Sneezing

The tradition of blessing sneezers is composed of several superstitions. First, there is heart superstition. The old stories say when you sneeze your heart momentarily stops beating. So, you have to bless a person who sneezed to kick-start their frozen heart.

Who in the hell believes this shit? No one has ever died from a sneeze. A sneeze has never been the cause of death. What if you had allergies and you sneezed like thirty times in a row? Wouldn't you need CPR?

The second superstition involves Satan. They say the devil enters your body when you sneeze. You need a blessing to exorcise the devil before he sets up shop and corrupts your soul. Well what happens when you sneeze and nobody is around? You would have to track down a stranger to say "God bless you."

Imagine doing this while staying at a hotel and having to knock on the room next door in the middle of the night? The hotel would call the cops and get you kicked out. "But, officer, you don't understand. No one else was around to say 'God bless you.'"

I refuse to say "God bless you" when people sneeze. One time I was in line at the supermarket and a guy sneezed right next to me. I was totally silent and that pissed him off.

"Thank you!" He said in a snarky voice.

"I didn't say a word," I replied.

"I know. You're supposed to say, 'God bless you!'"

"I just met you. I'm not giving you the Lord's blessing, okay? You might have molested a kid an hour ago."

Salty Luck

"Don't spill the salt, that's bad luck!"

That's another superstition involving Satan. If you spill the salt, the devil gets pissed off and comes after you. When that happens, you're supposed to throw some of the spilled salt over your left shoulder really quick. The devil always attacks from the rear and on the left side. So, if you throw it over your left shoulder, it hits the devil in the eyes and then he can't put a hex on you.

I'm not making this shit up! This is the explanation for the salt superstition. Ok, let's suspend disbelief and go with this theory. Don't you think after all these years he would switch things up? One day he would say to himself, "I'm sick of getting salt in my eyes; I'm going to attack from the right side this time!"

"You know what? Fuck it. I'm coming from the right side this time! Or better yet I'm going to wear goggles next time!"

I was on a date with this girl one time. It was our first date and during dinner, I spilled the salt on the table.

"Throw it over your left shoulder," she said. "Because it's going to be bad luck if you don't!"

"I'm not doing that," I said.

"Well, something bad is going to happen to you then."

"No, that's all right. I'm going to take a pass."

She finally dropped it but I was worried I might have pissed her off. Then, she blew me in the car on the way home. The superstition is nonsense. Since I didn't throw the salt, I was supposed to have bad luck. Getting road head on a first date is amazing luck, but she didn't swallow. So, when she wrote down her phone number for me I threw it over my left shoulder out the car window.

Awful Traditions: New Year's Eve

New Year's Eve blows!

We just celebrated Christmas and all the bullshit that comes with that, you'd think it would be a good time for a real break. But, less than a week later, we have to deal with stupid New Year's Eve. It's a worthless tradition, which boils down to a bunch of amateurs staying out all night and drinking until they puke. What an awful way to start the year!

Also, there's a lot of pressure because of the New Year's Eve parties. There's always a party where you're forced to hang with a bunch of assholes you barely know. Or, you have to go to some douchey club. You're dreading the evening and your girlfriend is freaked out because she doesn't know what to wear.

Even if you go to a nice restaurant, you can only get an early reservation. All the other times are booked a year in advance. Even if you get in, you can't stay there for five hours waiting on midnight. So, you have to waste time until the fucking ball drops in Times Square. There is nothing special about a ball sliding down a fucking pole. Who gives a fuck? Besides, this same ball will drop again next year. Why does it matter if you miss it? Go on YouTube and watch it in the morning if it means that much to you.

When you're young, it makes sense to go wild on New Year's Eve. At that age, you don't care about getting drunk and sleeping in a doorway, under a bush, or in the backseat of a car next to a nice steaming pile of puke! You don't worry about wasting $300 on a hotel room. When you're older, New Year's Eve is a fucking pain in the ass!

The New Year's Eve Outfit

Like I said, women stress over their New Year's Eve outfits. It seems like every chick needs a new dress for the occasion. Even if she got four new ones for Christmas, she will still go out and buy a new one to wear one time. If you plan to attend a party for New Year's Eve, getting dressed with a woman is maddening!

"What's everybody else wearing at the party?"

"I guess . . . clothes?"

"Well, did any of your guy friends say what they're wearing or what their girlfriends are wearing?"

"No. That would probably be the last thing I talk to them about."

"Well, what are you going to wear?"

"I haven't even thought about it. If we have to leave the house at 6:45 p.m. that night I'll figure it out at about 6:35 p.m."

"I'm just asking to get a general idea of what everyone will be wearing."

"It'll be something between a pair of sweats and a gown. Does that help?"

"Well, can you find out for sure?"

"No. What if we didn't know anyone, what would you wear?"

"Fucking asshole!"

SLAM! The bathroom door closes on your face! Sounds like it's going to be a fun night, huh?

It doesn't matter what she wears since it won't fit because she's been eating garbage holiday food for two weeks. That makes her miserable. She's bloated from all the cake and ice cream she shoveled down her throat and needs reassurance from you she still looks good. Now, you have to lie your ass off.

"Do I look fat to you?"

"Compared to who?"

"Did I put weight on? I feel fat. I shouldn't have eaten so much over the holidays. Would you tell me if I was fat? Just be honest with me. I look way too fat in this, don't I?"

If you're a man and you find yourself in this situation take the fifth like you're getting questioned by the police and you're waiting for your lawyer to arrive. Just shut your mouth and let her ramble on, eventually she'll calm down and turn her attention to you and your clothes.

"You're going to wear that?"

"Yeah."

"I don't know if that is something you want to wear to a New Year's Eve party."

Again, don't argue. Don't comment! At this point, you'll be thinking about saying something real mean.

Something like, "I'm going to make sure there is enough air in the tires, so we don't have a blowout on the way to the party since you gained a lot weight recently!"

Yay! Happy Fucking New Year!

Rehashing Resolutions

New Year's resolutions are another awful thing I hate! If people wanted to change, they wouldn't wait until the first day of the year. Why do you have to start on January 1? Start now, whatever day it is!

Honestly, it doesn't matter the day, nobody sticks with the resolutions. Even though they swear, they will make big changes!

"No, this year is going to be to be different."

NO, NOTHING IS GOING TO BE DIFFERENT!

Your list of resolutions is a fantasy! Don't bother writing one this year. You don't have to because I've already written one for you.

Florentine's Awful Resolution List

This year . . .

You will not change your job.

You will not get out of that bad relationship you're in.

You will not spend more time with friends and family.

You will not be nicer to your spouse.

You will not cut back on drinking.

You will not cut back on shopping.

You will not pay off your credit cards.

You will not have the balls to ask for that raise at work.

You will not give up coffee.

You will not cut back on sugar.

You will not start the paleo diet.

You will not read more books this year.

You will not take more walks.

You will not start that garden you always wanted to start.

You will not do anything on your fucking corny bucket list.

You will not start charity work.

You will not work in the soup kitchen.

You will not go back to church.

You will not have a garage sale in the spring.

You will not get down to your high school weight.

You will not take an interest in your significant other's hobbies.

Stop lying to yourself! None of this shit will happen and if you can accept that, you won't walk around feeling awful next year.

The only thing that will change this year is how you write the date. You need to change the year by one digit. That's it!

Accept that you're a procrastinator and you're not doing a damn thing to change your life! Enjoy your New Year's Eve. Have a few cocktails, hopefully get laid, and when you wake up take a nice big shit in the morning! That's how you start the New Year right!

THE AWFUL AFTERWORD

If you've read this far, you've read more books than me. Congratulations!

Here's the thing. You just read hundreds of pages about shit I hate. Facebook Freaks. Instagram Exhibitionists. Distracted Drivers. Shitty Superstitions.

But know this, I don't hate everything!

I say this because some people take things so personally that they forget what it means to make fun of things. I'm a comedian and I've learned that the best humor is found in *tension*. The tension between what you think is right and what I think is wrong. When we argue about those things we can walk away wounded and pissed off, or we can accept our disagreements and find the humor right in the center of our biggest differences.

One guy confronted me the other day.

"Florentine, you're a fucking asshole! I use to love ketchup but you made fun of it, and said it was only for kids, and now I can't eat it without feeling like an idiot. You've ruined ketchup for me!"

Don't let anyone change your mind about the things you love! If it isn't obvious by now, I love heavy metal. If someone made fun of me for loving metal, it wouldn't change a damn thing. Okay, this dude doesn't like heavy metal. I'm not going to run home and throw away all my heavy metal albums or my vast collection of concert T-shirts. Fuck no!

Put things in perspective—we have to laugh about shit that annoys us because life throws a lot of awful shit our way. Sometimes it's hard to have fun at all, so we have to take advantage of every opportunity to do it while we can.

If any of this gets under your skin. Let it go, relax, and laugh!

Most of all, be yourself. Just remember what I titled this book *Everybody Is Awful (Except You!)*. You're not awful, it's the other guy, and we are all hilarious motherfuckers!

ACKNOWLEDGMENTS

I want to thank my manager Jonathan Brandstein. It's coming up on twelve years and counting that I'm lucky to have the best manager in the business. Julia Buchwald for believing in a creep like me. Jud Laghi for getting this nonsense together and getting it sold as a book. Mark Jones for all your hard work shaping this book up and stopping me from looking like an illiterate ass. Chris Laker and Myka Fox for helping me get these ramblings of a madman into book form. Mike Berkowitz, Marcus Levy, Danielle Esparza, and everyone at APA agency. Pete Pappalardo, Rick Dorfman, and Tony Burton. Don Jamieson for being my partner in crime the last two decades. Eddie Trunk for getting us two clowns on *That Metal Show* and having a blast for seven years. My family for believing in me since day one: Joe, Bob, Dan, Dianne, Linda, and Kathy. My mom, who is the strongest person I've ever met. I love you. All my nieces and nephews: Danny, Erica, Joey, Lia, Elyse, Paula, Jenna, Tom, Mike, George, Joseph, and also Big George, Bruce, Fran, Trish. My comic friends who make me laugh every day: Jim Norton, Keith Robinson, Rich Vos, Bob Levy, Vinnie Brand, Eric McMahon, Chad Zumock, Joe Howard, Chuck Mignanelli, Artie Fletcher, Artie Lange, Dean Delray, Bill Burr, Robert Kelly, Lenny Marcus, Kevin Brennan, Kate

Quigley, Rachel Feinstein, Amy Schumer, Marina Franklin, Nikki Glaser, Bonnie McFarlane, Morgan Murphy, Mike Morse, Nick Diapolo, Laura Levitis, Colin Quinn, Craig Gass. My dirt-bag friends: Gary from Fla, Tom Jannarone, Tony Bondi, Kevin Corrigan, Steve Iskowitz, Gary Bradley, Tim O'Neill, Scott Capizanno, Rudy Sarzo, Scott Crocco, Chuck Crocco, Club Soda Kenny, Dave from Fla, Brian Hyland, John Pavlick, Marc Labelle, Dan The Song Parody Man, Steve Schott, Steve Mohn, Brian Slagel, Joe Tetro. I want to thank the following radio shows around the country for having me on whenever I came to town: Opie and Anthony, Johnny Dare, Paul and Young Ron, Todd and Tyler, Ron Bennington, Tom Bernard, *The Woody Show,* Rover, Mike Calta, Sid Rosenberg, Bubba The Love Sponge, Scott Ferrall, Kidd Chris, Preston and Steve, Angelo Cataldi, *98 Rock Morning Show* in Baltimore, The Regular Guys, Pugs N Kelly, *Waking Up to the Wolf, The Rizzuto Show,* Gooch at 92.3 Komp, Bob & Tom, Shredd & Ragan, Jeff Zito, *The Monsters in the Morning,* and of course, Howard Stern. He is the sole reason my career took off and if it wasn't for him believing in me I would be selling used cars for a living today. RIP Uncle Donald, Mrs. Balzano, Otto and George, Lemmy.

I want to thank my ex-wife for giving me the gift of my son Luke. There is no greater joy in the world than what I get from that kid every day. (Well, maybe if the original Black Sabbath did one last show together.) He is an amazing human being and I hope one day when he reads this book he will not feel the same rage his dad has! Haha!